IDEAS HAVE CONSEQUENCES

IDEAS HAVE CONSEQUENCES

EXPANDED EDITION

Richard M. Weaver

The University of Chicago Press
Chicago and London

Richard M. Weaver (1910–63) was an American scholar, revered twentieth-century conservative, and professor of English and rhetoric at the University of Chicago. He is the author of several books, including *The Ethics of Rhetoric* and *Visions of Order: The Cultural Crisis of Our Time*.

The University of Chicago Press, Chicago 60637
The University of Chicago Press, Ltd., London
© 1948, 2013 by The University of Chicago
Foreword © 2013 by Roger Kimball
All rights reserved. Published 2013.
Printed in the United States of America

23 22 21 20 19 18 17 16 15 14   1 2 3 4 5

ISBN-13: 978-0-226-09006-1 (paper)
ISBN-13: 978-0-226-09023-8 (e-book)

DOI: 10.7208/chicago/9780226090238.001.0001

An earlier version of the foreword appeared as "The Consequences of Richard Weaver" by Roger Kimball in *The New Criterion*, September 2006.

The afterword was originally published in *Steps toward Restoration: The Consequences of Richard Weaver's Ideas*, edited by Ted J. Smith III (ISI Books, 1998), pp. 1–33. Reprinted by permission of ISI Books.

Library of Congress Cataloging-in-Publication Data

Weaver, Richard M., 1910–1963, author.
    Ideas have consequences / Richard M. Weaver. — Expanded edition.
    pages cm
    Includes bibliographical references.
    ISBN 978-0-226-09006-1 (paperback : alkaline paper) —
ISBN 978-0-226-09023-8 (e-book)   1. Civilization—Philosophy.
I. Title.
    CB19.W4 2013
    901—dc23

                                                        2013019828

♾ This paper meets the requirements of ANSI/NISO Z39.48-1992 (Permanence of Paper).

CONTENTS

THE CONSEQUENCES OF RICHARD WEAVER

By Roger Kimball

The past shows unvaryingly that when a people's freedom disappears, it goes not with a bang, but in silence amid the comfort of being cared for. That is the dire peril in the present trend toward statism. If freedom is not found accompanied by a willingness to resist, and to reject favors, rather than to give up what is intangible but precarious, it will not long be found at all.

RICHARD WEAVER, 1962

The simple process of preserving our present civilization is supremely complex, and demands incalculably subtle powers.

ORTEGA Y GASSET, 1930

In the great pantheon of half-forgotten conservative sages, the southern writer Richard M. Weaver (1910–63) occupies an important, if curious, niche. I say "writer," but that is an imprecise designation. By trade, Weaver was a professor of rhetoric. He is even the author of a textbook on the subject. One friend said that Weaver was "a rhetor doing the work of a philosopher." It might be more accurate to say that he was a critic doing the work of a prophet. Prophets as a species tend to specialize in bad news; they rarely return from the mountain reporting that the management has concluded that everything down below is just fine.

Weaver was no exception to this rule. He made his reputation as a latter-day Isaiah, bearing admonitory tidings to an inattentive populace. Above all, perhaps, he was an acolyte of what he lovingly called "lost causes." The fact that a cause had lost, he argued, did not necessarily rob it of nobility; it did not mean that we could not learn something from the ideals that inspired it; it did not even mean that, ultimately, it was really lost. For what is lost might also be regained. It might serve not only as a reminder but also as a model, a new goal. In the "longer run," as Weaver put it, what seemed lost might eventually prove victorious.

Such, anyway, were among the explicit rationales that Weaver offered about the value of lost causes. An additional attraction, I suspect, lay in the romance of defeat. "Things reveal themselves passing away": Weaver liked to quote that Yeatsian line. I believe he cherished the passing away as much as the accompanying revelation.

Weaver the man was—or became—almost as eccentric as his work. Born in North Carolina, he was the first of four children. His father, an outgoing man who owned a livery stable, died when Richard was only six and his mother was expecting her last child. The family eventually resettled in Lexington, Kentucky, where his mother managed Embry and Company, a millinery business owned by her brother. Although Weaver became a formidable debater, he was a shy, bookish boy: his sister Polly remembers him sequestered in his bedroom for hours on end with the family typewriter. He blossomed socially in college, though his intellectual vocation seems to have settled upon him only gradually. In an autobiographical essay called "Up From Liberalism" (1958), Weaver recalls that in his undergraduate years at the University of Kentucky earnest professors had him "persuaded entirely that the future was with science, liberalism, and equalitarianism." By the time he graduated, in 1932, the Great Depression had swept the country and Weaver, like many others, had evolved into a full-fledged Socialist. He served as secretary of the campus Socialist

Party and, during Norman Thomas's presidential campaign, rose to be secretary of the statewide Socialist Party.

His metanoia began at Vanderbilt where he came under the mesmerizing spell of John Crowe Ransom, the "subtle doctor" to whom he dedicated *The Southern Tradition at Bay*. First published in 1968, five years after Weaver's death, the book began life as a dissertation, completed in 1943 under the great critic Cleanth Brooks, about the postbellum American South, its literature, manners, and aspirations, rooted in the life before the Civil War. *The Southern Tradition at Bay* is a brilliant, complex, cranky work, part literary criticism, part social commentary, part hortatory injunction. "From the bleakness of a socialist bureaucracy," Weaver wrote in his peroration, "men will sooner or later turn to something stirring: they will decide again to live strenuously, or romantically." That was the ideal. The route to realizing it was to be found in the "Old South," which Weaver proposed as a co-conspirator in the pursuit of his strenuous, romantic oppositions.

As one of Weaver's biographers, Fred Douglas Young, notes, *The Southern Tradition at Bay* was less a dissertation than "an apologia." Most of Weaver's mature themes make their appearance in the book. Indeed, several critics have pointed out that Weaver's later work is essentially an elaboration and application of ideas he first formulated there. Weaver begins by laying out a constellation of four distinctively Southern, almost universally besieged, virtues: the feudal concept of society organized by an interlocking hierarchy of duties, filiations, and privileges; the code of chivalry; the ancient concept of the gentleman; and religion or at least "religiousness," which may have "little relation to creeds" but, prodded by "a sense of the inscrutable," "leaves man convinced of the existence of supernatural intelligence and power, and leads him to the acceptance of life as mystery."

But that scaffolding describes only one level of Weaver's argument. For every lost cause there is a victorious alternative. Weaver was interested in analyzing, elaborating, advocating what he took to be the virtues of the Old South; even more, he was interested in criticizing the forces that had undermined those virtues. The enemy, he thought, was not so much Grant's and Sherman's armies as the spirit that moved them. It was "science and technology." It was centralized government. It was the ethic of "total war." It was affluence, materialism, and the love of comfort. It was the demand for homogenization and equality, "a disorganizing concept," Weaver writes, "in so far as human relationships mean order." "Participation is open to all"—to this extent, he acknowledges, the doctrine of equality is sound. But "however we allow men to start in the world, we may be sure that as long as standards of quality exist, there will be a sorting out." It is the same with the relationship between the sexes: the demand for equality between the sexes, Weaver thought, was part of the decadence of our age. In a word, Weaver's enemy was modernity. Hence the lessons of America's premier lost cause: "The mind of the South," Weaver wrote, is "conspicuous for its resistance to the spiritual disintegration of the modern world." Is such resistance futile? Never mind. Resistance itself is glorious: strenuous, romantic, precisely because— perhaps one should say "even if"—it's futile.

Later, Weaver came to acknowledge that the South's resistance in modern America had all but collapsed. But yesterday, in the 1940s, it still seemed like a magnificent ruin: "a hall hung with splendid tapestries in which no one would care to live." They may be inhospitable. They may be strange and even rebarbative. Nevertheless, Weaver concludes, they offer essential existential wisdom: "From them we can learn something of how to live." The Old South, he declared (and the italics are his) was "*the last non-materialist civilization in the Western World.*"

Students of the period will instantly recognize *The Southern Tradition at Bay* as an homage to, an extension of, the spirit of the Southern Agrarians whose famous manifesto *I'll Take My Stand* had been published in 1930. Many of the movement's founding members—John Crowe Ransom, Allen Tate, Donald Davidson—

were among Weaver's mentors and friends. There is a lot of elegy in such writing, and not a little bitterness. Whatever the sins of the South, had not its punishment been excessive? The South had not so much been defeated as crushed by the Union armies: that was bad enough. Even worse were subsequent efforts to obliterate or efface Southern identity, to transform even its virtues into vices, its heroisms into crimes. "In short," as Weaver put it tartly in a later essay, "the South either had no history, or its history was tainted with slavery and rebellion and must be abjured." Weaver, like the Agrarians, abjured the abjuration.

What one might call the "localness" of the Southern Agarians' teaching—their emphasis on the importance of place, the genealogy of art and thought—began to wean Weaver from the centralizing imperatives of socialism. After taking a master's degree in 1937, he spent a restless few years teaching, first in Alabama, then Texas. It was while driving across the Texas prairies in 1939, he recalled later, that he had a revelation: "I did not have to go back to this job . . . I did not have to go on professing the clichés of liberalism, which were becoming meaningless to me. . . . At the end of that year I chucked the uncongenial job and went off to start my education over, being now arrived at the age of thirty."

Weaver now switched into high intellectual gear. At LSU he studied not only with Cleanth Brooks but also with such commanding figures as Robert Penn Warren and the literary historian Arlin Turner. Summers found him at Harvard, the Sorbonne, or the University of Virginia pursuing his studies. He finished his dissertation in 1943 and, recommended by Brooks, landed a job at the University of Chicago.

Weaver's entire career unfolded at the University of Chicago. He taught there from 1944 until his early death, from heart failure, in 1963 at the age of fifty-three. Weaver was dutiful—he always insisted on keeping his hand in teaching introductory courses when most senior staff fobbed off that chore on junior colleagues—but he was never happy in Chicago. One biographer speaks of his "hermetically sealed existence" there. He had colleagues, but few if any close friends. He never married. He lived alone in a small apartment with his pipe, his books, and a nightly beer for company. In the summer, he would go south to stay with his mother in the house he had bought her. He traveled there by train—he boarded an airplane only once in his life, to lecture in California; and he always instructed his mother to have the garden plowed by horse or mule, not—abomination of desolation—by a tractor.

There was more than a little irony in Weaver's situation. The great Henry Regnery, who published Weaver's book *The Ethics of Rhetoric* in 1953, summed it up with his customary aptitude. How odd that a man who repudiated the modern world and all its works should spend virtually his entire career "at a university founded by John D. Rockefeller, where, not long before he arrived, the first chain reaction had taken place . . . and in the city where fifteen years before there had been a great exposition, 'A Century of Progress,' celebrating achievements of science and technology." As Regnery noted, being so out of place must have been a powerful goad to Weaver's ire, and hence to his work.

Weaver's star rose dramatically in 1948 when *Ideas Have Consequences* was published by the University of Chicago Press. He instantly went from being just another disgruntled prof to being a sort of academic celebrity. He had a knack for telling people what they didn't want to hear in such a way that they craved to hear it. "This is another book," he began mournfully, "about the dissolution of the West." It was Weaver's constant theme. *Ideas* is a brief book, fewer than two hundred pages. But it crackles with passion and extensive, if sometimes imperfectly digested, erudition. Its success, or perhaps I should say its notoriety, astonished everyone, not least its author.

Paul Tillich—then at the height of his fame—spoke for one contingent when he declared the book "brilliantly written, daring, and radical. . . . It will shock, and philosophical shock is the beginning of wisdom." Others were less admiring. Writing in *The*

Antioch Review, one critic denounced Weaver as a "pompous fraud" and his book as a retreat to "a fairyland of absolute essences." *Ideas* was not a measured, carefully modulated argument; it did not elicit a measured, carefully modulated response. I suspect that some part of the book's success lay in its title. It is not catchy exactly, but it bluntly articulates an immovable intellectual truth: ideas do indeed have consequences. It is ironical, then, that Weaver intensely disliked the title, which was foisted upon him by his editor. In his excellent biography of Weaver, *Barbarians in the Saddle* (1997), Joseph Scotchie reports that Weaver almost pulled the book from the press over the title. Weaver's friend Russell Kirk said that *The Adverse Descent* was the title Weaver favored; other scholars say it was *The Fearful Descent*. Whatever it was, Weaver was fortunate that his editor prevailed.

As Weaver's friend Eliseo Vivas, a professor of philosophy, noted, Weaver's defining intellectual trait was "audacity of mind." It was audacity of a decidedly contrarian stamp. In the mid-1940s, when Weaver was writing *Ideas*, America was blooming with postwar prosperity. The ideology of progress was underwritten by the joy of victory and the extraordinary dynamo of capitalism suddenly unburdened by the demands of war. Material abundance was rendered even more seductive by a burgeoning technological revolution: cars, radios, gadgets galore. Easier. Faster. Louder. More—above all, more.

Weaver wanted none of it. *Ideas*, he said, was not a work of philosophy but "an intuition of a situation," namely, a situation in which the "world . . . has lost its center." Weaver traced that loss back to the rise of nominalism in the twelfth century, a familiar pedigree that is both accurate and comical. It is accurate because the modern world—a world deeply shaped by a commitment to scientific rationality—does have a root in the disabusing speculations of nominalism. It is comical because to locate the source of our present difficulties on so distant and so elevated a plane is simply to underscore our impotence. If William of Occam is responsible for what's wrong with the world, there's not much we can do about it.

Nevertheless, Weaver's diagnosis struck a chord, or rather many chords. On the strength of *Ideas*, the quirky Yale polemicist Willmoore Kendall declared Weaver "captain of the anti-liberal team"—a team, as Scotchie notes in *Barbarians in the Saddle*, that was only just coming into its own with figures like Weaver and Russell Kirk and, just over the horizon, William F. Buckley Jr. and the circle he assembled around *National Review* (a circle that included very public intellectuals like James Burnham and Russell Kirk, as well as more reticent figures like Weaver).

In fact, though, Weaver was not so much antiliberal as antimodern. This shows itself, for example, in his discussion of private property. He praises private property as "the last metaphysical right." But although he clearly appreciates the place of private property in fostering liberty and forestalling the tyranny of the state, his defense is actually highly qualified: "Respecters of private property are really obligated to oppose much that is done today in the name of private enterprise, for corporate organization and monopoly are the very means whereby property is casting aside its privacy." Private property is good, Weaver thinks, so long as it is limited: "The moral solution is the distributive ownership of small properties." Who or what oversees that distribution was not a problem he solves.

Something similar can be said about his discussion of total war, war conducted not just among recognized combatants but against civilians as well. No sane person is "in favor" of war, total or otherwise. But Weaver's laments about the loss of chivalry in war are bootless. Weaver locates the origin of total war in the American Civil War and the North's brutal campaign against the South. But he applies his criticism to other conflicts—for example, the firebombing of Dresden and the use of the atomic bomb in Japan. In the posthumously published *Visions of Order* (1964), he argues that the usual justification—that those actions ultimately "saved lives"—has "a fatal internal contradiction," since if one really wanted to save lives one could simply capitulate and stop fighting. Really, though, there is no contradiction. It takes away nothing of the horror of those episodes to say that the *real* alternative—for example, invading the Japanese islands—would have been even more horrible. The decision about saving lives was made *then*, in the aftermath of Iwo Jima and Okinawa. The point is that the choices life presents us with, especially in wartime, are often not between good and bad but between bad and worse. That is a central conservative insight, and it is a curious feature of Weaver's thought that, despite his ostensible celebration of the particular over the abstract, he sometimes sacrifices vital human reality for the sake of an abstraction.

Weaver's taxonomy of decadence is both bracing and overstated—bracing, perhaps, because overstated. He lamented "the lowering of standards, the adulteration of quality, and, in general, . . . the loss of those things which are essential to the life of civility and culture." Who can disagree? In his opening pages, he notes that "Man is constantly being assured today that he has more power than ever before in history, but his daily experience is one of powerlessness." This is certainly true, and it testifies to the accuracy of de Tocqueville's analysis of "democratic despotism," which does not tyrannize so much as it enervates and infantilizes. But then Weaver proceeds to argue that if one "is with a business organization, the odds are great that he has sacrificed every other kind of independence in return for that dubious one known as financial. Modern social and corporate organization makes independence an expensive thing; in fact, it may make common integrity a prohibitive luxury for the ordinary man." Is this true?

Weaver acknowledged at the beginning of *Ideas* that lamentation about "the decadence of a present age is one of the permanent illusions of mankind." But that was a pro forma rider. At the center of his analysis was the insistence that modern man, "like Macbeth," had made an evil decision to trade allegiance to transcendent principles for present gain. From this Faustian bargain all manner of bad things flow. Weaver warns about "the insolence of material success," the "technification of the world," the obliteration of distinctions that make living "strenuously, or romantically" possible. "Presentism," the effort to begin each day, as Allen Tate put it, as if there were no yesterday, has robbed man of his history and therefore his identity as a moral agent. Weaver is particularly harsh on what he regards as the tepid ambitions of the middle class: "Loving comfort, risking little, terrified by the thought of change, its aim is to establish a materialistic civilization which will banish threats to its complacency."

Abetting this establishment is what Weaver calls the "Great Stereopticon," the "wonderful machine" constructed by "the vested interests of our age" in order to enforce the society's addiction to spiritual conformity and material comfort above the more tonic values of traditional culture. "It is the function of this machine," Weaver writes, "to project selected pictures of life in the hope that what is seen will be imitated. All of us in the West who are within the long reach of technology are sitting in the audience. We are told the time to laugh and the time to cry, and signs are not wanting that the audience grows ever more responsive to its cues." Media culture—Weaver cites newspapers, the movies, and radio (imagine what he would have said about television!)—is a primary instrument employed by the Great Stereopticon for keeping the populace on the surface of life and not "breaking through to deeper significances." There was not a lot about contemporary culture that Weaver applauded. In a chapter called "Egotism in Work and Art" he launches an extraordinary, racially tinged attack on jazz, "the clearest of all signs of our age's deep-seated predilection for barbarism."[1]

In all this, I think, Weaver's analysis is not so much wrong as radically incomplete. He speaks of "hysterical optimism," and rightly; it is not, however, the only form of hysteria on offer. Irving Kristol famously said that a neoconservative is a liberal mugged by reality. Weaver might be described as a Socialist repelled by modernity. You don't have to be Karl Marx to recognize that capitalism is a powerful solvent of tradition. Moralists have inveighed against luxury ever since there was luxury to tempt us. But capitalism and the free markets which feed it drastically ups the ante. Capitalism is an unparalleled engine of wealth. It is also an unparalleled engine of freedom, but that freedom has two faces: increased choice and increased dislocation. Weaver lamented the latter and blamed the former.

Weaver has said his "core belief" revolved around the recognition that "man in this world cannot make his will his law without any regard to limits and to the fixed nature of things." Quite right, and Weaver has penetrating things to say about the "spoiled child psychology" that underlies the modern culture of entitlement. He is right, too, that modern science and technology present us with formidable moral temptations. But the pretense that we might issue a categorical no to modernity would not only be impracticable, but it would also be immoral—and it would be so on good Weaverian grounds. Richard Weaver was eloquent in warning about the disastrous results of Prometheanism, of attempting to subjugate the world to our will. But part—a large part—of our world today is the world shaped by science. What greater hubris than to think we could dispense with that world in an effort to live "strenuously, or romantically"?

In a way, the work of Richard Weaver is not unlike the Old South he memorialized. It, too, is a splendidly appointed but, for most of us, an uninhabitable domicile. Still, it is one we cannot simply repudiate without diminishment. Weaver's work is a heady, sometimes an impossible stew. But it is one from which we can learn "something of how to live" or (what is almost the same thing) something of how not to.

FOREWORD

When *Ideas Have Consequences* was published in 1948, it met a response far beyond anything anticipated by the author. The book was written in the period immediately following the Second World War, and it was in a way a reaction to that war—to its immense destructiveness, to the strain it placed upon ethical principles, and to the tensions it left in place of the peace and order that were professedly sought.

Its rhetorical note may perhaps be explained by this, but many people have written me to say that they found their own thoughts expressed in the book. I have therefore tried to understand its appeal by asking myself whether it can really be considered a work of philosophy. It is a work of philosophy to the extent that it tries to analyze many features of modern disintegration by referring them to a first cause. This was a change that overtook the dominant philosophical thinking of the West in the fourteenth century, when the reality of transcendentals was first seriously challenged. To many readers this has been the most unsatisfactory part of the reasoning; but to others it has, seemingly, been the most convincing. I will merely say that something like this is necessary if one believes in the primacy of ideas. I was attempting a rigorous cause-and-effect analysis of the decline of belief in standards and values, and there must be a starting point.

I have come to feel increasingly, however, that it is not primarily a work of philosophy; it is rather an intuition of a situation. The intuition is of a world which has lost its center, which desires to believe again in value and obligation. But this world is not willing to realize how it has lost its belief or to face what it must accept in order to regain faith in an order of goods. The dilemma is very widely felt, and I image this accounts for the interest of the book to many persons who would not be at all happy with the political implications of some of the conclusions.

In a more general revision I would very probably change a few matters of emphasis and try to find less topical applications for some of the ideas. But I see no reason, after the lapse of more than a decade, to retreat from the general position of social criticism. It seems to me that the world is now more than ever dominated by the gods of mass and speed and that the worship of these can lead only to the lowering of standards, the adulteration of quality, and, in general, to the loss of those things which are essential to the life of civility and culture. The tendency to look with suspicion upon excellence, both intellectual and moral, as "undemocratic" shows no sign of diminishing.

The book was intended as a challenge to forces that threaten the foundations of civilization, and I am very happy to see it appear in a more accessible edition.

Richard M. Weaver

INTRODUCTION

This is another book about the dissolution of the West. I attempt two things not commonly found in the growing literature of this subject. First, I present an account of that decline based not on analogy but on deduction. It is here the assumption that the world is intelligible and that man is free and that those consequences we are now expiating are the product not of biological or other necessity but of unintelligent choice. Second, I go so far as to propound, if not a whole solution, at least the beginning of one, in the belief that man should not follow a scientific analysis with a plea of moral impotence.

In considering the world to which these matters are addressed, I have been chiefly impressed by the difficulty of getting certain initial facts admitted. This difficulty is due in part to the widely prevailing Whig theory of history, with its belief that the most advanced point in time represents the point of highest development, aided no doubt by theories of evolution which suggest to the uncritical a kind of necessary passage from simple to complex. Yet the real trouble is found to lie deeper than this. It is the appalling problem, when one comes to actual cases, of getting men to distinguish between better and worse. Are people today provided with a sufficiently rational scale of values to attach these predicates with intelligence? There is ground for declaring that modern man has become a moral idiot. So few are those who care to examine their lives, or to accept the rebuke which comes of admitting that our present state may be a fallen state, that one questions whether people now understand what is meant by the superiority of an ideal. One might expect abstract reasoning to be lost upon them; but what is he to think when attestations of the most concrete kind are set before them, and they are still powerless to mark a difference or to draw a lesson? For four centuries every man has been not only his own priest but his own professor of ethics, and the consequence is an anarchy which threatens even that minimum consensus of value necessary to the political state.

Surely we are justified in saying of our time: If you seek the monument to our folly, look about you. In our own day we have seen cities obliterated and ancient faiths stricken. We may well ask, in the words of Matthew, whether we are not faced with "great tribulation, such as was not since the beginning of the world." We have for many years moved with a brash confidence that man had achieved a position of independence which rendered the ancient restraints needless. Now, in the first half of the twentieth century, at the height of modern progress, we behold unprecedented outbreaks of hatred and violence; we have seen whole nations desolated by war and turned into penal camps by their conquerors; we find half of mankind looking upon the other half as criminal. Everywhere occur symptoms of mass psychosis. Most portentous of all, there appear diverging bases of value, so that our single planetary globe is mocked by worlds of different understanding. These signs of disintegration arouse fear, and fear leads to desperate unilateral efforts toward survival, which only forward the process.

Like Macbeth, Western man made an evil decision, which has become the efficient and final cause of other evil decisions. Have we forgotten our encounter with the witches on the heath? It occurred in the late fourteenth century, and what the witches said to the protagonist of this drama was that man could realize himself more fully if he would only abandon his belief in the existence of transcendentals. The powers of darkness were working subtly, as always, and they couched this proposition in the seemingly innocent form of an attack upon universals. The defeat of logical realism in the great medieval debate was the crucial event in the history of Western culture; from this flowed those acts which issue now in modern decadence.

One may be accused here of oversimplifying the historical process, but I take the view that the conscious policies of men and governments are not mere rationalizations of what has been brought about by unaccountable forces. They are rather deductions from our most basic ideas of human destiny, and they have a great, though not unobstructed, power to determine our course.

For this reason I turn to William of Occam as the best representative of a change which came over man's conception of reality at this historic juncture. It was William of Occam who propounded the fateful doctrine of nominalism, which denies that universals have a real existence. His triumph tended to leave universal terms mere names serving our convenience. The issue ultimately involved is whether there is a source of truth higher than, and independent of, man; and the answer to the question is decisive for one's view of the nature and destiny of humankind. The practical result of nominalist philosophy is to banish the reality which is perceived by the intellect and to posit as reality that which is perceived by the senses. With this change in the affirmation of what is real, the whole orientation of culture takes a turn, and we are on the road to modern empiricism.

It is easy to be blind to the significance of a change because it is remote in time and abstract in character. Those who have not discovered that world view is the most important thing about a man, as about the men composing a culture, should consider the train of circumstances which have with perfect logic proceeded from this. The denial of universals carries with it the denial of everything transcending experience. The denial of everything transcending experience means inevitably—though ways are found to hedge on this—the denial of truth. With the denial of objective truth there is no escape from the relativism of "man the measure of all things." The witches spoke with the habitual equivocation of oracles when they told man that by this easy choice he might realize himself more fully, for they were actually initiating a course which cuts one off from reality. Thus began the "abomination of desolation" appearing today as a feeling of alienation from all fixed truth.

Because a change of belief so profound eventually influences every concept, there emerged before long a new doctrine of nature. Whereas nature had formerly been regarded as imitating a transcendent model and as constituting an imperfect reality, it was henceforth looked upon as containing the principles of its own constitution and behavior. Such revision has had two important consequences for philosophical inquiry. First, it encouraged a careful study of nature, which has come to be known as science, on the supposition that by her acts she revealed her essence. Second, and by the same operation, it did away with the doctrine of forms imperfectly realized. Aristotle had recognized an element of unintelligibility in the world, but the view of nature as a rational mechanism expelled this element. The expulsion of the element of unintelligibility in nature was followed by the abandonment of the doctrine of original sin. If physical nature is the totality and if man is of nature, it is impossible to think of him as suffering from constitutional evil; his defections must now be attributed to his simple ignorance or to some kind of social deprivation. One comes thus by clear deduction to the corollary of the natural goodness of man.

And the end is not yet. If nature is a self-operating mechanism and man is a rational animal adequate to his needs, it is next in order to elevate rationalism to the rank of a philosophy. Since man proposed now not to go beyond the world, it was proper that he should regard as his highest intellectual vocation methods of interpreting data supplied by the senses. There followed the transition to Hobbes and Locke and the eighteenth-century rationalists, who taught that man needed only to reason correctly upon evidence from nature. The question of what the world was made for now becomes meaningless because the asking of it presupposes something prior to nature in the order of existents. Thus it is not the mysterious fact of the world's existence which interests the new man but explanations of how the world works. This is the rational basis for modern science, whose systemization of phenomena is, as Bacon declared in the *New Atlantis*, a means to dominion.

At this stage religion begins to assume an ambiguous dignity, and the question of whether it can endure at all in a world of rationalism and science has to be faced. One solution was deism, which makes God the outcome of a rational reading of nature. But this religion, like all those which deny antecedent truth, was powerless to bind; it merely left each man to make what he could of the world open to the senses. There followed references to "nature and nature's God," and the anomaly of a "humanized" religion.

Materialism loomed next on the horizon, for it was implicit in what had already been framed. Thus it soon became imperative to explain man by his environment, which was the work of Darwin and others in the nineteenth century (it is further significant of the pervasive character of these changes that several other students were arriving at similar explanations when Darwin published in 1859). If man came into this century trailing clouds of transcendental glory, he was now accounted for in a way that would satisfy the positivists.

With the human being thus firmly ensconced in nature, it at once became necessary to question the fundamental character of his motivation. Biological necessity, issuing in the survival of the fittest, was offered as the *causa causans*, after the important question of human origin had been decided in favor of scientific materialism.

After it has been granted that man is molded entirely by environmental pressures, one is obligated to extend the same theory of causality to his institutions. The social philosophers of the nineteenth century found in Darwin powerful support for their thesis that human beings act always out of economic incentives, and it was they who completed the abolishment of freedom of the will. The great pageant of history thus became reducible to the economic endeavors of individuals and classes; and elaborate prognoses were constructed on the theory of economic conflict and resolution. Man created in the divine image, the protagonist of a great drama in which his soul was at stake, was replaced by man the wealth-seeking and-consuming animal.

Finally came psychological behaviorism, which denied not only freedom of the will but even such elementary means of direction as instinct. Because the scandalous nature of this theory is quickly apparent, it failed to win converts in such numbers as the others; yet it is only a logical extension of them and should in fairness be embraced by the upholders of material causation. Essentially, it is a reduction to absurdity of the line of reasoning which began when man bade a cheerful goodbye to the concept of transcendence.

There is no term proper to describe the condition in which he is now left unless it be "abysmality." He is in the deep and dark abysm, and he has nothing with which to raise himself. His life is practice without theory. As problems crowd upon him, he deepens confusion by meeting them with *ad hoc* policies. Secretly he hungers for truth but consoles himself with the thought that life should be experimental. He sees his institutions crumbling and rationalizes with talk of emancipation. Wars have to be fought, seemingly with increased frequency; therefore he revives the old ideals—ideals which his present assumptions actually render meaningless—and, by the machinery of state, forces them again to do service. He struggles with the paradox that total immersion in matter unfits him to deal with the problems of matter.

His decline can be represented as a long series of abdications. He has found less and less ground for authority at the same time he thought he was setting himself up as the center of authority in the universe; indeed, there seems to exist here a dialectic process which takes away his power in proportion as he demonstrates that his independence entitles him to power. This story is eloquently reflected in changes that have come over education. The shift from the truth of the intellect to the facts of experience followed hard upon the meeting with the witches. A little sign appears, "a cloud no bigger than a man's hand," in a change that came over the study of logic in the fourteenth century—the century of Occam. Logic became grammaticized, passing from a science which taught men *vere loqui* to one which taught *recte loqui* or from an ontological division by categories to a study of signification, with the inevitable focus upon historical meanings. Here begins the assault upon definition: if words no longer correspond to objective realities, it seems no great wrong to take liberties with words. From this point on, faith in language as a means of arriving at truth weakens, until our own age, filled with an acute sense of doubt, looks for a remedy in the new science of semantics.

So with the subject matter of education. The Renaissance increasingly adapted its course of study to produce a successful man of the world, though it did not leave him without philosophy and the graces, for it was still, by heritage, at least, an ideational world and was therefore near enough transcendental conceptions to perceive the dehumanizing effects of specialization. In the seventeenth century physical discovery paved the way for the incorporation of the sciences, although it was not until the nineteenth that these began to challenge the very continuance of the ancient intellectual disciplines. And in this period the change gained momentum, aided by two developments of overwhelming influence. The first was a patent increase in man's dominion over nature which dazzled all but the most thoughtful; and the second was the growing mandate for popular education. The latter might have proved a good in itself, but it was wrecked on equalitarian democracy's unsolvable problem of authority: none was in a position to say what the hungering multitudes were to be fed. Finally, in an abject surrender to the situation, in an abdication of the authority of knowledge, came the elective system. This was followed by a carnival of specialism, professionalism, and vocationalism, often fostered and protected by strange bureaucratic devices, so that on the honored name of university there traded a weird congeries of interests, not a few of which were anti-intellectual even in their pretensions. Institutions of learning did not check but rather contributed to the decline by losing interest in *Homo sapiens* to develop *Homo faber*.

Studies pass into habits, and it is easy to see these changes reflected in the dominant type of leader from epoch to epoch. In the seventeenth century it was, on the one side, the royalist and learned defender of the faith and, on the other, aristocratic intellectuals of the type of John Milton and the Puritan theocrats who settled New England. The next century saw the domination of the Whigs in England and the rise of encyclopedists and romanticists on the Continent, men who were not without intellectual background but who assiduously cut the mooring strings to reality as they succumbed to the delusion that man is by nature good. Frederick the Great's rebuke to a sentimentalist, "*Ach, mein lieber Sulzer, er kennt nicht diese verdammte Rasse,*" epitomizes the difference between the two outlooks. The next period witnessed the rise of the popular leader and demagogue, the typical foe of privilege, who broadened the franchise in England, wrought revolution on the Continent, and in the United States replaced the social order which the Founding Fathers had contemplated with demagogism and the urban political machine. The twentieth century ushered in the leader of the masses, though at this point there occurs a split whose deep significance we shall have occasion to note. The new prophets of reform divide sharply into sentimental humanitarians and an elite group of remorseless theorists who pride themselves on their freedom from sentimentality. Hating this world they never made, after its debauchery of centuries, the modern Communists— revolutionaries and logicians—move toward intellectual rigor. In their decision lies the sharpest reproach yet to the desertion of intellect by Renaissance man and his successors. Nothing is more disturbing to modern men of the West than the logical clarity with which the Communists face all problems. Who shall say that this feeling is not born of a deep apprehension that here are the first true realists in hundreds of years and that no dodging about in the excluded middle will save Western liberalism?

This story of man's passage from religious or philosophical transcendentalism has been told many times, and, since it has usually been told as a story of progress, it is extremely difficult today to get people in any number to see contrary implications. Yet to establish the fact of decadence is the most pressing duty of our time because, until we have demonstrated that cultural decline is a historical fact—which can be established—and that modern man has about squandered his estate, we cannot combat those who have fallen prey to hysterical optimism.

Such is the task, and our most serious obstacle is that people traveling this downward path develop an insensibility which increases with their degradation. Loss is perceived most clearly at the beginning; after habit becomes implanted, one beholds the anomalous situation of apathy mounting as the moral crisis deepens. It is when the first faint warnings come that one has the best chance to save himself; and this, I suspect, explains why medieval thinkers were extremely agitated over questions which seem to us today without point or relevance. If one goes on, the monitory voices fade out, and it is not impossible for him to reach a state in which his entire moral orientation is lost. Thus in the face of the enormous brutality of our age we seem unable to make appropriate response to perversions of truth and acts of bestiality. Multiplying instances show complacency in the presence of contradiction which denies the heritage of Greece, and a callousness to suffering which denies the spirit of Christianity. Particularly since the great wars do we observe this insentience. We approach a condition in which we shall be amoral without the capacity to perceive it and degraded without means to measure our descent.

That is why, when we reflect upon the cataclysms of the age, we are chiefly impressed with the failure of men to rise to the challenge of them. In the past, great calamities have called forth, if not great virtues, at least heroic postures; but after the awful judgments pronounced against men and nations in recent decades, we detect notes of triviality and travesty. A strange disparity has developed between the drama of these actions and the conduct of the protagonists, and we have the feeling of watching actors who do not comprehend their roles.

Hysterical optimism will prevail until the world again admits the existence of tragedy, and it cannot admit the existence of tragedy until it again distinguishes between good and evil. Hope of restoration depends upon recovery of the "ceremony of innocence," of that clearness of vision and knowledge of form which enable us to sense what is alien or destructive, what does not comport with our moral ambition. The time to seek this is now, before we have acquired the perfect insouciance of those who prefer perdition. For, as the course goes on, the movement turns centrifugal; we rejoice in our abandon and are never so full of the sense of accomplishment as when we have struck some bulwark of our culture a deadly blow.

In view of these circumstances, it is no matter for surprise that, when we ask people even to consider the possibility of decadence, we meet incredulity and resentment. We must consider that we are in effect asking for a confession of guilt and an acceptance of sterner obligation; we are making demands in the name of the ideal or the suprapersonal, and we cannot expect a more cordial welcome than disturbers of complacency have received in any other age. On the contrary, our welcome will rather be less today, for a century and a half of bourgeois ascendancy has produced a type of mind highly unreceptive to unsettling thoughts. Added to this is the egotism of modern man, fed by many springs, which will scarcely permit the humility needed for self-criticism.

The apostles of modernism usually begin their retort with catalogues of modern achievement, not realizing that here they bear witness to their immersion in particulars. We must remind them that we cannot begin to enumerate until we have defined what is to be sought or proved. It will not suffice to point out the inventions and processes of our century unless it can be shown that they are something other than a splendid efflorescence of decay. Whoever desires to praise some modern achievement should wait until he has related it to the professed aims of our civilization as rigorously as the Schoolmen related a corollary to their doctrine of the nature of God. All demonstrations lacking this are pointless.

If it can be agreed, however, that we are to talk about ends before means, we may begin by asking some perfectly commonplace questions about the condition of modern man. Let us, first of all, inquire whether he knows more or is, on the whole, wiser than his predecessors.

This is a weighty consideration, and if the claim of the modern to know more is correct, our criticism falls to the ground, for it is hardly to be imagined that a people who have been gaining in knowledge over the centuries have chosen an evil course.

Naturally everything depends on what we mean by knowledge. I shall adhere to the classic proposition that there is no knowledge at the level of sensation, that therefore knowledge is of universals, and that whatever we know as a truth enables us to predict. The process of learning involves interpretation, and the fewer particulars we require in order to arrive at our generalization, the more apt pupils we are in the school of wisdom.

The whole tendency of modern thought, one might say its whole moral impulse, is to keep the individual busy with endless induction. Since the time of Bacon the world has been running away from, rather than toward, first principles, so that, on the verbal level, we see "fact" substituted for "truth," and on the philosophic level, we witness attack upon abstract ideas and speculative inquiry. The unexpressed assumption of empiricism is that experience will tell us what we are experiencing. In the popular arena one can tell from certain newspaper columns and radio programs that the average man has become imbued with this notion and imagines that an industrious acquisition of particulars will render him a man of knowledge. With what pathetic trust does he recite his facts! He has been told that knowledge is power, and knowledge consists of a great many small things.

Thus the shift from speculative inquiry to investigation of experience has left modern man so swamped with multiplicities that he no longer sees his way. By this we understand Goethe's dictum that one may be said to know much only in the sense that he knows little. If our contemporary belongs to a profession, he may be able to describe some tiny bit of the world with minute fidelity, but still he lacks understanding. There can be no truth under a program of separate sciences, and his thinking will be invalidated as soon as *ab extra* relationships are introduced.

The world of "modern" knowledge is like the universe of Eddington, expanding by diffusion until it approaches the point of nullity.

What the defenders of present civilization usually mean when they say that modern man is better educated than his forebears is that he is literate in larger numbers. The literacy can be demonstrated; yet one may question whether there has ever been a more deceptive panacea, and we are compelled, after a hundred years of experience, to echo Nietzsche's bitter observation: "Everyone being allowed to learn to read, ruineth in the long run not only writing but also thinking." It is not what people can read; it is what they do read, and what they can be made, by any imaginable means, to learn from what they read, that determine the issue of this noble experiment. We have given them a technique of acquisition; how much comfort can we take in the way they employ it? In a society where expression is free and popularity is rewarded they read mostly that which debauches them and they are continuously exposed to manipulation by controllers of the printing machine—as I shall seek to make clear in a later passage. It may be doubted whether one person in three draws what may be correctly termed knowledge from his freely chosen reading matter. The staggering number of facts to which he today has access serves only to draw him away from consideration of first principles, so that his orientation becomes peripheral. And looming above all as a reminder of this fatuity is the tragedy of modern Germany, the one totally literate nation.

Now those who side with the Baconians in preferring shoes to philosophy will answer that this is an idle complaint, because the true glory of modern civilization is that man has perfected his material estate to a point at which he is provided for. And probably it could be shown statistically that the average man today, in countries not desolated by war, has more things to consume than his forebears. On this, however, there are two important comments to be made.

The first is that since modern man has not defined his way of life, he initiates himself into an endless series when he enters the struggle for an "adequate" living. One of the strangest disparities of history lies between the sense of abundance felt by older and simpler societies and the sense of scarcity felt by the ostensibly richer societies of today. Charles Péguy has referred to modern man's feeling of "slow economic strangulation," his sense of never having enough to meet the requirements which his pattern of life imposes on him. Standards of consumption which he cannot meet, and which he does not need to meet, come virtually in the guise of duties. As the abundance for simple living is replaced by the scarcity for complex living, it seems that in some way not yet explained we have formalized prosperity until it is for most people only a figment of the imagination. Certainly the case of the Baconians is not won until it has been proved that the substitution of covetousness for wantlessness, of an ascending spiral of desires for a stable requirement of necessities, leads to the happier condition.

Suppose, however, we ignore this feeling of frustration and turn our attention to the fact that, by comparison, modern man has more. This very circumstance sets up a conflict, for it is a constant law of human nature that the more a man has to indulge in, the less disposed he is to endure the discipline of toil—that is to say, the less willing he is to produce that which is to be consumed. Labor ceases to be functional in life; it becomes something that is grudgingly traded for that competence, or that superfluity, which everyone has a "right" to. A society spoiled in this manner may be compared to a drunkard: the more he imbibes the less is he able to work and acquire the means to indulge his habit. A great material establishment, by its very temptation to luxuriousness, unfits the owner for the labor necessary to maintain it, as has been observed countless times in the histories of individuals and of nations.

But let us waive all particular considerations of this sort and ask whether modern man, for reasons apparent or obscure, feels an increased happiness. We must avoid superficial conceptions of this state and look for something fundamental. I should be willing to accept Aristotle's "feeling of conscious vitality." Does he feel equal to life; does he look upon it as does a strong man upon a race?

First, one must take into account the deep psychic anxiety, the extraordinary prevalence of neurosis, which make our age unique. The typical modern has the look of the hunted. He senses that we have lost our grip upon reality. This, in turn, produces disintegration, and disintegration leaves impossible that kind of reasonable prediction by which men, in eras of sanity, are able to order their lives. And the fear accompanying it unlooses the great disorganizing force of hatred, so that states are threatened and wars ensue. Few men today feel certain that war will not wipe out their children's inheritance; and, even if this evil is held in abeyance, the individual does not rest easy, for he knows that the Juggernaut technology may twist or destroy the pattern of life he has made for himself. A creature designed to look before and after finds that to do the latter has gone out of fashion and that to do the former is becoming impossible.

Added to this is another deprivation. Man is constantly being assured today that he has more power than ever before in history, but his daily experience is one of powerlessness. Look at him today somewhere in the warren of a great city. If he is with a business organization, the odds are great that he has sacrificed every other kind of independence in return for that dubious one known as financial. Modern social and corporate organization makes independence an expensive thing; in fact, it may make common integrity a prohibitive luxury for the ordinary man, as Stuart Chase has shown. Not only is this man likely to be a slavey at his place of daily toil, but he is cribbed, cabined, and confined in countless ways, many of which are merely devices to make possible physically the living together of masses. Because these are deprivations of what is rightful, the end is frustration, and hence the look, upon the faces of those whose souls have not already become minuscule, of hunger and unhappiness.

These are some questions that should be put to the eulogists of progress. It will certainly be objected that the decadence of a present age is one of the permanent illusions of mankind; it will be said that each generation feels it with reference to the next in the same way that parents can never quite trust the competence of their children to deal with the great world. In reply we must affirm that, given the conditions described, each successive generation does show decline in the sense that it stands one step nearer the abysm. When change is in progress, every generation will average an extent of it, and that some cultures have passed from a high state of organization to dissolution can be demonstrated as objectively as anything in history. One has only to think of Greece, of Venice, of Germany. The assertion that changes from generation to generation are illusory and that there exist only cycles of biological reproduction is another form of that denial of standards, and ultimately of knowledge, which lies at the source of our degradation.

Civilization has been an intermittent phenomenon; to this truth we have allowed ourselves to be blinded by the insolence of material success. Many late societies have displayed a pyrotechnic brilliance and a capacity for refined sensation far beyond anything seen in their days of vigor. That such things may exist and yet work against that state of character concerned with choice, which is the anchor of society, is the great lesson to be learned.

In the final reach of analysis our problem is how to recover that intellectual integrity which enables men to perceive the order of goods. The opening chapter, therefore, attempts to set forth the ultimate source of our feeling and thinking about the world, which makes our judgments of life not shifting and casual but necessary and right.

1

The Unsentimental Sentiment

But the thing a man does practically believe (and this is often
enough without asserting it even to himself, much less to others);
the thing a man does practically lay to heart, and know for certain,
concerning his vital relations to this mysterious Universe, and his
duty and destiny there, that is in all cases the primary thing for him,
and creatively determines all the rest.

CARLYLE

Every man participating in a culture has three levels of conscious
reflection: his specific ideas about things, his general beliefs or
convictions, and his metaphysical dream of the world.

The first of these are the thoughts he employs in the activity of
daily living; they direct his disposition of immediate matters and,
so, constitute his worldliness. One can exist on this level alone
for limited periods, though pure worldliness must eventually bring
disharmony and conflict.

Above this lies his body of beliefs, some of which may be heri-
tages simply, but others of which he will have acquired in the ordinary course of his reflection. Even the simplest souls define a few
rudimentary conceptions about the world, which they repeatedly
apply as choices present themselves. These, too, however, rest on
something more general.

Surmounting all is an intuitive feeling about the immanent nature of reality, and this is the sanction to which both ideas and beliefs are ultimately referred for verification. Without the metaphysical dream it is impossible to think of men living together harmoniously over an extent of time. The dream carries with it an evaluation, which is the bond of spiritual community.

When we affirm that philosophy begins with wonder, we are affirming in effect that sentiment is anterior to reason. We do not undertake to reason about anything until we have been drawn to it by an affective interest. In the cultural life of man, therefore, the fact of paramount importance about anyone is his attitude toward the world. How frequently it is brought to our attention that nothing good can be done if the will is wrong! Reason alone fails to justify itself. Not without cause has the devil been called the prince of lawyers, and not by accident are Shakespeare's villains good reasoners. If the disposition is wrong, reason increases maleficence; if it is right, reason orders and furthers the good. We have no authority to argue anything of a social or political nature unless we have shown by our primary volition that we approve some aspects of the existing world. The position is arbitrary in the sense that here is a proposition behind which there stands no prior. We begin our other affirmations after a categorical statement that life and the world are to be cherished.

It appears, then, that culture is originally a matter of yea-saying, and thus we can understand why its most splendid flourishing stands often in proximity with the primitive phase of a people, in which there are powerful feelings of "oughtness" directed toward the world, and before the failure of nerve has begun.

Simple approbation is the initial step only; a developed culture is a way of looking at the world through an aggregation of symbols, so that empirical facts take on significance and man feels that he is acting in a drama, in which the cruxes of decision sustain interest and maintain the tone of his being. For this reason a true culture cannot be content with a sentiment which is sentimental with regard to the world. There must be a source of clarification, of arrangement and hierarchy, which will provide grounds for the employment of the rational faculty. Now man first begins this clarification when he becomes mythologist, and Aristotle has noted the close relationship between myth-making and philosophy. This poetry of representation, depicting an ideal world, is a great cohesive force, binding whole peoples to the acceptance of a design and fusing their imaginative life. Afterward comes the philosopher, who points out the necessary connection between phenomena, yet who may, at the other end, leave the pedestrian level to talk about final destination.

Thus, in the reality of his existence, man is impelled from behind by the life-affirming sentiment and drawn forward by some conception of what he should be. The extent to which his life is shaped, in between these, by the conditions of the physical world is indeterminable, and so many supposed limitations have been transcended that we must at least allow the possibility that volition has some influence upon them.

The most important goal for one to arrive at is this imaginative picture of what is otherwise a brute empirical fact, the *donnée* of the world. His rational faculty will then be in the service of a vision which can preserve his sentiment from sentimentality. There is no significance to the sound and fury of his life, as of a stage tragedy, unless something is being affirmed by the complete action. And we can say of one as of the other that the action must be within bounds of reason if our feeling toward it is to be informed and proportioned, which is a way of saying, if it is to be just. The philosophically ignorant vitiate their own actions by failing to observe measure. This explains why precultural periods are characterized by formlessness and post-cultural by the clashing of forms. The darkling plain, swept by alarms, which threatens to be the world of our future, is an arena in which conflicting ideas, numerous after the accumulation of centuries, are freed from the discipline earlier imposed by ultimate conceptions. The decline is to confusion; we are agitated by sensation and look with wonder upon the serene somnambulistic creations of souls which had the metaphysical anchorage. Our ideas become convenient perceptions, and we accept contradiction because we no longer feel the necessity of relating thoughts to the metaphysical dream.

It must be apparent that logic depends upon the dream, and not the dream upon it. We must admit this when we realize that logical processes rest ultimately on classification, that classification is by identification, and that identification is intuitive. It follows then that a waning of the dream results in confusion of counsel, such as we behold on all sides in our time. Whether we describe this as decay of religion or loss of interest in metaphysics, the result is the same; for both are centers with power to integrate, and, if they give way, there begins a dispersion which never ends until the culture lies in fragments. There can be no doubt that the enormous exertions made by the Middle Ages to preserve a common world view—exertions which took forms incomprehensible to modern man because he does not understand what is always at stake under such circumstances—signified a greater awareness of realities than our leaders exhibit today. The Schoolmen understood that the question, *universalia ante rem* or *universalia post rem*, or the question of how many angels can stand on the point of a needle, so often cited as examples of Scholastic futility, had incalculable ramifications, so that, unless there was agreement upon these questions, unity in practical matters was impossible. For the answer supplied that with which they bound up their world; the ground of this answer was the fount of understanding and of evaluation; it gave the heuristic principle by which societies and arts could be approved and regulated. It made one's sentiment toward the world rational, with the result that it could be applied to situations without plunging man into sentimentality on the one hand or brutality on the other.

The imposition of this ideational pattern upon conduct relieves us of the direful recourse to pragmatic justification. Here, indeed, lies the beginning of self-control, which is a victory of transcendence. When a man chooses to follow something which is arbitrary as far as the uses of the world go, he is performing a feat of abstraction; he is recognizing the noumenal, and it is this, and not that self-flattery which takes the form of a study of his own achievements, that dignifies him.

Such is the wisdom of many oracular sayings: man loses himself in order to find himself; he conceptualizes in order to avoid an immersion in nature. It is our destiny to be faced originally with the world as our primary datum but not to end our course with only a wealth of sense impressions. In the same way that our cognition passes from a report of particular details to a knowledge of universals, so our sentiments pass from a welter of feeling to an illumined concept of what one ought to feel. This is what is known as refinement. Man is in the world to suffer his passion; but wisdom comes to his relief with an offer of conventions, which shape and elevate that passion. The task of the creators of culture is to furnish the molds and the frames to resist that "sinking in upon the moral being" which comes of accepting raw experience. Without the transcendental truth of mythology and metaphysics, that task is impossible. One imagines that Jacob Burckhardt had a similar thought in mind when he said, "Yet there remains with us the feeling that all poetry and all intellectual life were once the handmaids of the holy, and have passed through the temple."

The man of self-control is he who can consistently perform the feat of abstraction. He is therefore trained to see things under the aspect of eternity, because form is the enduring part. Thus we invariably find in the man of true culture a deep respect for forms. He approaches even those he does not understand with awareness that a deep thought lies in an old observance. Such respect distinguishes him from the barbarian, on the one hand, and the degenerate, on the other. The truth can be expressed in another way by saying that the man of culture has a sense of style. Style requires measure, whether in space or time, for measure imparts structure, and it is structure which is essential to intellectual apprehension. That it does not matter what a man believes is a statement heard on every side today. The statement carries a fearful implication. If a man is a philosopher in the sense with which we started, what he believes tells him what the world is for. How can men who disagree about what the world is for agree about any of the minutiae of daily conduct? The statement really means that it does not matter what a man believes so long as he does not take his beliefs seriously. Anyone can observe that this is the status to which religious belief has been reduced for many years. But suppose he does take his beliefs seriously? Then what he believes places a stamp upon his experience, and he belongs to a culture, which is a league founded on exclusive principles. To become eligible, one must be able to say the right words about the right things, which signifies in turn that one must be a man of correct sentiments. This phrase, so dear to the eighteenth century, carries us back to the last age that saw sentiment and reason in a proper partnership.

That culture is sentiment refined and measured by intellect becomes clear as we turn our attention to a kind of barbarism appearing in our midst and carrying unmistakable power to disintegrate. This threat is best described as the desire of immediacy, for its aim is to dissolve the formal aspects of everything and to get at the supposititious reality behind them. It is characteristic of the barbarian, whether he appears in a precultural stage or emerges from below into the waning day of a civilization, to insist upon seeing a thing "as it is." The desire testifies that he has nothing in himself with which to spiritualize it; the relation is one of thing to thing without the intercession of imagination. Impatient of the veiling with which the man of higher type gives the world imaginative meaning, the barbarian and the Philistine, who is the barbarian living amid culture, demands the access of immediacy. Where the former wishes representation, the latter insists upon starkness of materiality, suspecting rightly that forms will mean restraint. There is no need to speak of Vandals and Goths; since our concern is with the "vertical invasion of the barbarians" in our own time, I shall cite an instance from the modern period—and from the United States, so symbolical of the world of the future.

The American frontiersman was a type who emancipated himself from culture by abandoning the settled institutions of the seaboard and the European motherland. Reveling in the new absence of restraint, he associated all kinds of forms with the machinery of oppression which he had fled and was now preparing to oppose politically. His emancipation left him impatient of symbolism, of indirect methods, and even of those inclosures of privacy which all civilized communities respect. De Tocqueville made the following observation of such freedmen: "As it is on their own testimony that they are accustomed to rely, they like to discern the object which engages their attention with extreme clearness; they therefore strip off as much as possible all that covers it, they rid themselves of whatever separates them from it, they remove whatever conceals it from sight, in order to view it more closely in the broad light of day. This disposition of mind soon leads them to contemn forms, which they regard as useless and inconvenient veils placed between them and the truth."

The frontiersman was seeking a solvent of forms, and he found his spokesmen in such writers as Mark Twain, a large part of whose work is simply a satire upon the more formal European way of doing things. As the impulse moved eastward, it encouraged a belief that the formal was the outmoded or at least the un-American. A plebeian distrust of forms, flowering in eulogies of plainness, became the characteristic American mentality.

Has America vulgarized Europe, or has Europe corrupted America? There is no answer to this question, for each has in its own way yielded to the same impulse. Europe long ago began the expenditure of its great inheritance of medieval forms, so that Burke, in the late eighteenth century, was sharply aware that the "unbought grace of life" was disappearing. America is responsible for the vulgarization of the Old World only in the sense that, like a forcing house, it brought the impulses to fruition sooner. It enjoys the dubious honor of a foremost place in the procession. Today over the entire world there are dangerous signs that culture, as such, is marked for attack because its formal requirements stand in the way of expression of the natural man.

Many cannot conceive why form should be allowed to impede the expression of honest hearts. The reason lies in one of the limitations imposed upon man: unformed expression is ever tending toward ignorance. Good intention is primary, but it is not enough: that is the lesson of the experiment of romanticism.

The member of a culture, on the other hand, purposely avoids the relationship of immediacy; he wants the object somehow depicted and fictionized, or, as Schopenhauer expressed it, he wants not the thing but the idea of the thing. He is embarrassed when this is taken out of its context of proper sentiments and presented bare, for he feels that this is a reintrusion of that world which his whole conscious effort has sought to banish. Forms and conventions are the ladder of ascent. And hence the speechlessness of the man of culture when he beholds the barbarian tearing aside some veil which is half adornment, half concealment. He understands what is being done, but he cannot convey the understanding because he cannot convey the idea of sacrilege. His cries of *abeste profani* are not heard by those who in the exhilaration of breaking some restraint feel that they are extending the boundaries of power or of knowledge.

Every group regarding itself as emancipated is convinced that its predecessors were fearful of reality. It looks upon euphemisms and all the veils of decency with which things were previously draped as obstructions which it, with superior wisdom and praiseworthy courage, will now strip away. Imagination and indirection it identifies with obscurantism; the mediate is an enemy to freedom. One can see this in even a brief lapse of time; how the man of today looks with derision upon the prohibitions of the 1890's and supposes that the violation of them has been without penalty! He would suffer poignant disillusion had he a clear enough pattern in his soul to be able to measure differences; but one consequence of this debauchery, as we shall see, is that man loses discrimination. For, when these veils are stripped aside, we find no reality behind them, or, at best, we find a reality of such commonplaceness that we would willingly undo our little act of brashness. Those will realize, who are capable of reflection, that the reality which excites us is an idea, of which the indirection, the veiling, the withholding, is part. It is our various supposals about a matter which give it meaning, and not some intrinsic property which can be seized in the barehanded fashion of the barbarian. In a wonderfully prescient passage Burke foretold the results of such positivism when it was first unleashed by the French Revolution: "All the pleasing illusions, which made power gentle and obedience liberal, which harmonized the different shades of life, and which, by a bland assimilation, incorporated into politics the sentiments which beautify and soften private society, are to be dissolved by this new conquering empire of light and reason. All the decent drapery of life is to be rudely torn off. All the superadded ideas, furnished from the wardrobe of a moral imagination, which the heart owns, and the understanding ratifies, as necessary to cover the defects of our naked, shivering nature, and to raise it to dignity in our own estimation, are to be exploded as a ridiculous, absurd, and antiquated fashion."

Barbarism and Philistinism cannot see that knowledge of material reality is a knowledge of death. The desire to get ever closer to the source of physical sensation—this is the downward pull which puts an end to ideational life No education is worthy of the name which fails to make the point that the world is best understood from a certain distance or that the most elementary understanding requires a degree of abstraction. To insist on less is to merge ourselves with the exterior reality or to capitulate to the endless induction of empiricism.

Our age provides many examples of the ravages of immediacy, the clearest of which is the failure of the modern mind to recognize obscenity. This failure is not connected with the decay of puritanism. The word is employed here in its original sense to describe that which should be enacted off-stage because it is unfit for public exhibition. Such actions, it must be emphasized, may have no relation to gross animal functions; they include intense suffering and humiliation, which the Greeks, with habitual perspicacity and humanity, banned from their theater. The Elizabethans, on the other hand, with their robust allusions to the animal conditions of man's existence, were none the less not obscene. It is all in the way one touches this subject.

This failure of the concept of obscenity has been concurrent with the rise of the institution of publicity which, ever seeking to widen its field in accordance with the canon of progress, makes a virtue of desecration. In the nineteenth century this change came visibly over the world, bringing expressions of concern from people who had been brought up in the tradition of proper sentiment. Propriety, like other old-fashioned anchorages, was abandoned because it inhibited something. Proud of its shamelessness, the new journalism served up in swaggering style matter which heretofore had been veiled in decent taciturnity. It was natural that so true an apostle of culture as Matthew Arnold should have sensed the mortal enemy in this. After a tour of the United States in 1888, he recorded his conviction that "if one were searching for the best means to efface and kill in a whole nation the discipline of self-respect, the feeling for what is elevated, he could do no better than take the American newspapers." Is this why, two hundred years before, a governor of Virginia had thanked God, to the scandal of succeeding generations, that there was not a newspaper in the colony? Have we here another example of the evil discerned most clearly on its first appearance? What he beheld in germ has grown so immeasurably that today we have media of publicity which actually specialize in the kind of obscenity which the cultivated, not the prurient, find repugnant, and which the wisest of the ancients forbade.

In any case, it has been left to the world of science and rationalism to make a business of purveying of the private and the offensive. Picture magazines and tabloid newspapers place before the millions scenes and facts which violate every definition of humanity. How common is it today to see upon the front page of some organ destined for a hundred thousand homes the agonized face of a child run over in the street, the dying expression of a woman crushed by a subway train, tableaux of execution, scenes of intense private grief. These are the obscenities. The rise of sensational journalism everywhere testifies to man's loss of points of reference, to his determination to enjoy the forbidden in the name of freedom. All reserve is being sacrificed to titillation. The extremes of passion and suffering are served up to enliven the breakfast table or to lighten the boredom of an evening at home. The area of privacy has been abandoned because the definition of person has been lost; there is no longer a standard by which to judge what belongs to the individual man. Behind the offense lies the repudiation of sentiment in favor of immediacy.

There are arguments founded upon insidious plausibility which seem to vindicate this publicizing. It is contended that such material is the raw stuff of life, and that it is the duty of organs of public information to leave no one deceived about the real nature of the world. The assertion that this is the real world begs the most important question of all. The raw stuff of life is precisely what the civilized man desires to have refined, or presented in a humane framework, for which sentiment alone can afford the support. The sensations purveyed by the press are admittedly for the demos, which is careless of understanding but avid of thrills. We shall have occasion to observe in many connections that one of the great conspiracies against philosophy and civilization, a conspiracy immensely aided by technology, is just this substitution of sensation for reflection. The machine cannot be a respecter of sentiment, and it was no accident that the great parade of obscenity followed hard upon the technification of our world.

It is inevitable that the decay of sentiment should be accompanied by a deterioration of human relationships, both those of the family and those of friendly association, because the passion for immediacy concentrates upon the presently advantageous. After all, there is nothing but sentiment to bind us to the very old or to the very young. Burke saw this point when he said that those who have no concern for their ancestors will, by simple application of the same rule, have none for their descendants. The decision of modern man to live in the here and now is reflected in the neglect of aging parents, whom proper sentiment once kept in positions of honor and authority. There was a time when the elder generation was cherished because it represented the past; now it is avoided and thrust out of sight for the same reason. Children are liabilities. As man becomes more immersed in time and material gratifications, belief in the continuum of race fades, and not all the tinkering of sociologists can put homes together again.

It is sometimes said when this point is brought up that urban living renders relationships of the older kind impossible. There can be little doubt of the truth of the proposition, but the very fact that it is put forward as apologia is an evidence of perversity. For motive is the decisive thing, and had our view of the world remained just, congested urban living, harmful in many other ways too, would not have become the pattern. The objectification in sticks and stones of our conception of living can hardly be pleaded as cause of that conception. When people set the highest value on relationships to one another, it does not take them long to find material accommodations for these. One is dealing here, as at every other point, with our estimate of the good life.

In Megalopolis the sentiment of friendship wastes away. Friends become, in the vulgarism of modern speech, "pals," who may be defined as persons whom your work compels you to associate with or, on a still more debased level, persons who will allow you to use them to your advantage. The meeting of minds, the sympathy between personalities which all cultured communities have regarded as part of the good life, demand too much sentiment for a world of machines and a false egalitarianism, and one detects even a faint suspicion that friendship, because it rests upon selection, is undemocratic. It is this type of mentality which will study with perfect naïveté a work on how to win friends and influence people. To one brought up in a society spiritually fused—what I shall call the metaphysical community—the idea of a campaign to win friends must be incomprehensible. Friends are attracted by one's personality, if it is of the right sort, and any conscious attempt is inseparable from guile. And the art of manipulating personalities obviously presumes a disrespect for personality. Only in a splintered community, where the spirit is starved to the point of atrophy, could such an imposture flourish.

When the primordial sentiments of a people weaken, there invariably follows a decline of belief in the hero. To see the significance of this, we must realize that the hero can never be a relativist. Consider for a moment the traditional soldier (not one of the automatons that comprise modern armies) as hero. It may at first seem paradoxical to say that he is of all members of the laity farthest removed from pragmatism; yet his is an absolute calling. Give him prudential motives, and he at once turns into a Falstaff. His service is to causes which are formulated as ideals, and these he is taught to hold above both property and life, as ceremonies of military consecration make plain. One sees this truth well exemplified in the extreme formalization of the soldier's conduct, a formalization which is carried into the chaos of battle; a well-drilled army moving into action is an imposition of maximum order upon maximum disorder. Thus the historical soldier is by genus not the blind, unreasoning agent of destruction which some contemporary writers make him out to be. He is rather the defender of the *ultima ratio*, the last protector of reason. Any undertaking that entails sacrifice of life has implications of transcendence, and the preference of death to other forms of defeat, to the "fate worse than death," is, on the secular level, the highest example of dedication. There seems little doubt that the ancient solidarity of priest and soldier—a solidarity becoming impossible today, now that mechanized mass warfare has removed soldiering from the realm of ethical significance—rests upon this foundation.

In addition, the disappearance of the heroic ideal is always accompanied by the growth of commercialism. There is a cause-and-effect relation here, for the man of commerce is by the nature of things a relativist; his mind is constantly on the fluctuating values of the market place, and there is no surer way for him to fail than to dogmatize and moralize about things. "Business and sentiment do not mix" is an adage of utmost significance. It explains the tendency of all organic societies to exclude the trader from positions of influence and prestige; it accounts, I am sure, for Plato's strictures on retail merchants in the *Laws*. The empirical character of British philosophy cannot be unrelated to the commercial habit of a great trading nation.

Some form of sentiment, deriving from our orientation toward the world, lies at the base of all congeniality. Vanishing, it leaves cities and nations mere empirical communities, which are but people living together in one place, without friendship or common understanding, and without capacity, when the test comes, to pull together for survival. On the other side is the metaphysical community, suffused with a common feeling about the world which enables all vocations to meet without embarrassment and to enjoy the strength that comes of common tendency. Our plea then must be to have back our metaphysical dream that we may save ourselves from the sins of sentimentality and brutality. Does not its absence explain why

The best lack all conviction, while the worst
Are full of passionate intensity?[1]

Without this grand source of ordering, our intensities turn to
senseless affection and drain us, or to hatreds and consume us. On
the one hand is sentimentality, with its emotion lavished upon the
trivial and the absurd; on the other is brutality, which can make
no distinctions in the application of its violence. Ages which have
borne reputations for cruelty are more to be regarded than those
renowned, as ours is coming to be, for brutality, because cruelty
is refined and, at least, discriminates its objects and intentions.
The terrible brutalities of democratic war have demonstrated how
little the mass mind is capable of seeing the virtue of selection and
restraint. The refusal to see distinction between babe and adult,
between the sexes, between combatant and noncombatant—distinctions which lay at the core of chivalry—the determination to
weld all into a formless unit of mass and weight—this is the destruction of society through brutality. The roar of the machine is
followed by the chorus of violence; and the accumulation of riches,
to which states dedicated themselves, is lost in a blind fanaticism
of destruction. Those who based their lives on the unintelligence of
sentimentality fight to save themselves with the unintelligence of
brutality.

The only redemption lies in restraint imposed by idea; but our
ideas, if they are not to worsen the confusion, must be harmonized
by some vision. Our task is much like finding the relationship between faith and reason for an age that does not know the meaning
of faith.

2

Distinction and Hierarchy

> For if all things had come into being in this automatic fashion, in-
> stead of being the outcome of mind, they would all be uniform and
> without distinction.
>
> ST. ATHANASIUS

The most portentous general event of our time is the steady obliteration of those distinctions which create society. Rational society is a mirror of the logos, and this means that it has a formal
structure which enables apprehension. The preservation of society
is therefore directly linked with the recovery of true knowledge.
For the success of our restoration it cannot be too often said that
society and mass are contradictory terms and that those who seek
to do things in the name of mass are the destroyers in our midst. If
society is something which can be understood, it must have structure; if it has structure, it must have hierarchy; against this metaphysical truth the declamations of the Jacobins break in vain.

Perhaps the most painful experience of modern consciousness
is the felt loss of center; yet, this is the inevitable result of centuries
of insistence that society yield its form. Anyone can observe that
people today are eager to know who is really entitled to authority,
that they are looking wistfully for the sources of genuine value.
In sum, they wish to know the truth, but they have been taught a

perversion which makes their chance of obtaining it less every day. This perversion is that in a just society there are no distinctions.

Our course has reached a point at which the question of whether man wishes to live in society at all or whether he wishes to live in a kind of animal relationship must be raised in all seriousness. For, if the proscription against every kind of distinction continues, there is no hope of integration except on the level of instinct.

After man evolves his metaphysical dream and becomes capable of rational sentiment, he recognizes two grounds of elevation, knowledge and virtue—if these are not one, which problem need not be decided here. The good man, the man with proved allegiance to correct sentiment, has been the natural trustee of authority; the man of knowledge has been necessary for such duties as require system and foresight. With these criteria it has been possible to erect a structure which mirrors our respect for value. In proportion to their contributions to the spiritual ideal which the creation expresses, men have found lodgment on the various levels, with the essential feeling that, since this structure is the logos, their stations were not arbitrary but natural and right. This is society, in which the human being has a sense of direction; literally, it might be said, he knows "up" from "down," because he knows where the higher goods are to be looked for. It is possible for him to live on the plane of spirit and intelligence because some points of reference are fixed.

Obviously this is not a social situation in which everyone is called Joe—that anonymous name so eloquent of modern man's feeling about people. If sentiment endures, there will be real names and even honorifics. For the good of all, prerogative will attach to higher functions, and this will mean hierarchy. But hierarchy requires a common assumption about ends, and that is why the competing ideologies of our age produce confusion.

The history of our social disintegration began with the unfixing of relationships in the fourteenth century, but the effort to do away with society entirely did not become programmatic until the nineteenth, when it appeared as a culmination of the prevailing nature philosophy. Since both knowledge and virtue require the concept of transcendence, they are really obnoxious to those committed to material standards, and we have seen how insistent was the impulse to look to the lower levels for guidance. Into social thinking there now enters a statistical unit, the consumer, which has the power to destroy utterly that metaphysical structure supporting hierarchy. Let us remember that traditional society was organized around king and priest, soldier and poet, peasant and artisan. Now distinctions of vocation fade out, and the new organization, if such it may be termed, is to be around capacities to consume. Underlying the shift is the theory of romanticism; if we attach more significance to feeling than to thinking, we shall soon, by a simple extension, attach more to wanting than to deserving. Even institutions of learning have yielded to the utilitarian standard, and former President James B. Conant of Harvard University declared in an address that the chief contribution of American universities had been the idea of equality of all useful labor.

This is the grand solution of socialism, which is itself the materialistic offspring of bourgeois capitalism.

It clarifies much to see that socialism is in origin a middle-class and not a proletarian concept. The middle class owes to its social location an especial fondness for security and complacency. Protected on either side by classes which must absorb shocks, it would forget the hazards of existence. The lower class, close to the reality of need, develops a manly fortitude and is sometimes touched with nobility in the face of its precariousness. The upper class bears responsibility and cannot avoid leading a life of drama because much is put into its hands. Lightnings of favor or of discontent flash in its direction, and he at the top of the hierarchy, whether it rests on true values or not, knows that he is playing for his head. In between lies the besotted middle class, grown enormous under the new orientation of Western man. Loving comfort, risking little, terrified by the thought of change, its aim is to establish a materialistic civilization which will banish threats to its complacency. It has conventions, not ideals; it is washed rather than clean. The plight of Europe today is the direct result of the bourgeois ascendancy and its corrupted world view.

Thus the final degradation of the Baconian philosophy is that knowledge becomes power in the service of appetite. The state, ceasing to express man's inner qualifications, turns into a vast bureaucracy designed to promote economic activity. It is little wonder that traditional values, however much they may be eulogized on commemorative occasions, today must dodge about and find themselves nooks and crannies if they are to survive at all. Burke's remark that the state is not "a partnership in things subservient only to gross animal existence" now seems as antiquated as his tribute to chivalry.

Upholders of tradition habitually classify the forces menacing our institutions as "subversive activity." The description is just. There is often in the language of ordinary people a logic which, for want of philosophy, they cannot interpret; and so is there here, for it can be shown that "subversive activity" has an exact application. Indeed, it would be difficult to find a more accurate phrase. The expression means plainly an inversion by which matter is placed over spirit or quantity placed over quality. Thus it describes perfectly what it is usually employed to describe—the various forms of collectivism which rest on a materialistic philosophy. The dullest member of a conservative legislative committee, seeking the source of threats to institutions, does not fail to see that those doctrines which exalt material interests over spiritual, to the confounding of rational distinctions among men, are positively incompatible with the society he is elected to represent. For expressing such views, he is likely to be condemned as ignorant or selfish, because normally he does not express them very well. Let us therefore find him a gifted spokesman. Here is Shakespeare on the subject of subversive activity:

> O, when degree is shak'd,
> Which is the ladder to all high designs,
> Then enterprise is sick! How could communities,
> Degrees in schools and brotherhoods in cities,
> Peaceful commerce from dividable shores,
> The primogenity and due of birth,
> Prerogative of age, crowns, sceptres, laurels,
> But by degree stand in authentic place?
> Take but degree away, untune that string,
> And hark what discord follows! Each thing meets
> In mere oppugnancy. The bounded waters
> Should lift their bosoms higher than the shores
> And make a sop of all this solid globe;
> Strength should be lord of imbecility,
> And the rude son should strike his father dead;
> Force should be right; or rather, right and wrong
> (Between whose endless jar justice resides)
> Should lose their names, and so should justice too.
> Then everything includes itself in power,
> Power into will, will into appetite;
> And appetite, an universal wolf,
> So doubly seconded with will and power,
> Must make perforce an universal prey,
> And last eat up himself.

And Milton, despite his fierce republicanism, seems to have agreed that "orders and degrees jar not with liberty, but well consist." Our legislator may find support, too, in the first book of Corinthians, in which Paul defends "diversities of operations." Paul offers the metaphysical argument:

> But now hath God set the members every one of them in the body, as it hath pleased him.
> And if they were all one member, where were the body?

The program of social democracy would take away this "ladder to all high designs." It would do so because high design is an extremely unsettling conception; it may involve arduous effort, self-denial, sleepless nights, all of which are repugnant to the bourgeoisie.[1] On the other hand, the goal of social democracy is scientific feeding.

If one dares to visualize the millennium of the social democrats, he is forced to picture a "healthy-minded," naturally good man, provided for by a paternalistic state and seeking to save himself from extinction by boredom through dabbling in some art. Is it any wonder that social democracy has never been able to motivate its programs? De Tocqueville was too shrewd to miss the connection: "Comfort becomes a goal when distinctions of rank are abolished and privileges destroyed."

Since subversive activity is the taking away of degree, it is logical that conservatives should treat as enemies all those who wish to abolish the sacred and secular grounds for distinctions among men. The proposal of the subverters is, however, impossible in practice, and the quarrel turns out to be over principles of selection. History thus far indicates that when the reformers get their turn, they merely substitute a bureaucratic hierarchy—and this because they discover that they do not wish society to collapse at all, but to continue under their conception of man's good.

The fight is being waged on all fronts, and the most insidious idea employed to break down society is an undefined equalitarianism. That this concept does not make sense even in the most elementary applications has proved no deterrent to its spread, and we shall have something to say later on about modern man's growing incapacity for logic. An American political writer of the last century, confronted with the statement that all men are created free and equal, asked whether it would not be more accurate to say that no man was ever created free and no two men ever created equal. Such hardheadedness would today be mistaken for frivolity. Thomas Jefferson, after his long apostleship to radicalism, made it the labor of his old age to create an educational system which would be a means of sorting out according to gifts and attainments.

Such equalitarianism is harmful because it always presents itself as a redress of injustice, whereas in truth it is the very opposite. I would mention here the fact, obvious to any candid observer, that "equality" is found most often in the mouths of those engaged in artful self-promotion. These secretly cherish the ladder to high designs but find that they can mount the lower rungs more easily by making use of the catchword. We do not necessarily grudge them their rise, but the concept they foster is fatal to the harmony of the world.

The comity of peoples in groups large or small rests not upon this chimerical notion of equality but upon fraternity, a concept which long antedates it in history because it goes immeasurably deeper in human sentiment. The ancient feeling of brotherhood carries obligations of which equality knows nothing. It calls for respect and protection, for brotherhood is status in family, and family is by nature hierarchical. It demands patience with little brother, and it may sternly exact duty of big brother. It places people in a network of sentiment, not of rights—that *hortus siccus* of modern vainglory.

It is eloquent of that loss of respect for logic to which we owe so many disasters that the French Revolution made equality and fraternity co-ordinates. In so doing, it offered a foretaste of the contemporary political campaign, which shamelessly promises everything.

Equality is a disorganizing concept in so far as human relationships mean order. It is order without a design; it attempts a meaningless and profitless regimentation of what has been ordered from time immemorial by the scheme of things. No society can rightly offer less than equality before the law; but there can be no equality of condition between youth and age or between the sexes; there cannot be equality even between friends. The rule is that each shall act where he is strong; the assignment of identical roles produces first confusion and then alienation, as we have increasing opportunity to observe. Not only is this disorganizing heresy busily confounding the most natural social groupings, it is also creating a reservoir of poisonous envy. How much of the frustration of the modern world proceeds from starting with the assumption that all are equal, finding that this cannot be so, and then having to realize that one can no longer fall back on the bond of fraternity!

However paradoxical it may seem, fraternity has existed in the most hierarchical organizations; it exists, as we have just noted, in that archetype of hierarchy, the family. The essence of co-operation is *congeniality*, the feeling of having been "born together." Fraternity directs attention to others, equality to self; and the passion for equality is simultaneous with the growth of egotism. The frame of duty which fraternity erects is itself the source of ideal conduct. Where men feel that society means station, the highest and the lowest see their endeavors contributing to a common end, and they are in harmony rather than in competition. It will be found as a general rule that those parts of the world which have talked least of equality have in the solid fact of their social life exhibited the greatest fraternity. Such was true of feudal Europe before people succumbed to various forms of the proposal that every man should be king. Nothing is more manifest than that as this social distance has diminished and all groups have moved nearer equality, suspicion and hostility have increased. In the present world there is little of trust and less of loyalty. People do not know what to expect of one another. Leaders will not lead, and servants will not serve.

It is a matter of common observation, too, that people meet most easily when they know their position. If their work and authority are defined, they can proceed on fixed assumptions and conduct themselves without embarassment toward inferior and superior. When the rule of equality obtains, however, no one knows where he belongs. Because he has been assured that he is "just as good as anybody else," he is likely to suspect that he is getting less than his deserts. Shakespeare concluded his wonderful discourse on degree with reference to "an envious fever." And when Mark Twain, in the role of Connecticut Yankee, undertook to destroy the hierarchy of Camelot, he was furious to find that serfs and others of the lower order were not resentful of their condition. He adopted then the typical Jacobin procedure of instilling hatred of all superiority. Resentment, as Richard Hertz has made plain, may well prove the dynamite which will finally wreck Western society.

The basis of an organic social order is fraternity uniting parts that are distinct. We must repeat, then, with reference to our first principles, that rebellion against distinction is an aspect of that world-wide and centuries-long movement against knowledge whose beginning goes back to nominalism. For it requires only a slight transference to say that, if our classifications of the world of physical nature are arbitrary, so, too, are those of human society. In other words, after we grant that those generalizations about the world which we necessarily make—and this is a necessity no one can really deny—do not express an objective order but only afford convenient modes, the same must be granted about society. With this conceded, inherent pattern is gone; nothing is justified that does not serve convenience, and there remains no court of appeal against subversion by pragmatism. Thus, repudiation of knowledge of *what is* destroys the basis of renewal. It is not fantastic but, rather, realistic to see as an ultimate result of this process the end of civilization.

It is generally assumed that the erasing of all distinctions will usher in the reign of pure democracy. But the inability of pure democracy to stand for something intelligible leaves it merely a verbal deception. If it promises equality before the law, it does no more than empires and monarchies have done and cannot use this as a ground to assert superiority. If it promises equality of condition, it promises injustice, because one law for the ox and the lion is tyranny. Pressure from the consumer instinct usually compels it to promise the latter. When it was found that equality before the law has no effect on inequalities of ability and achievement, humanitarians concluded that they had been tricked into asking only part of their just claim. The claim to political equality was then supplemented by the demand for economic democracy, which was to give substance to the ideal of the levelers. Nothing but a despotism could enforce anything so unrealistic, and this explains why modern governments dedicated to this program have become, under one guise and another, despotic. There are other aspects to the dilemma of radical egalitarianism. A defense often employed by the more sophisticated is that democratic equality allows each to develop his potentialities. This plausible argument involves grave questions about the nature of things. It is here implied that man is like a seed, having some immanent design of germination, so that for his flowering he needs that liberty which is "freedom from." If this is the whole account, it can only mean that our determination is naturalistic and that our growth is merely the unfolding of a plan established purely by nature. One need hardly add that this conception accepts orientation from below and assumes that man's destiny is to be natural, to develop like a plant. This makes impossible any thought of discipline, which would, under these circumstances, be a force constraining what nature had intended. But all teleology rejects "freedom from" in favor of "freedom to." That men are a field of wild flowers, naturally good in their growing, is the romantic fallacy.

A kindred notion is that democracy means opportunity for advancement, or in the language of the day, "a chance to be a success." Obviously this contention presumes hierarchy. The sort of advancement contemplated by these advocates is just the kind that requires a condition of high social organization, with rewards, degrees, and everything that comes with a frank recognition of superiority. If democracy means a chance to get ahead, it means a chance to rise above the less worthy, to have station with reference to points above and below. The solution of the dilemma is that these people wish democracy not as an end but as a means. Confronted with the realities described, the democrat may confess that his democracy is only a correction for a distorted aristocracy; he does want order, but he wants the kind in which the best, the gifted and the industrious, get ahead. There must be a fence, but the wrong rail is on top.

Notwithstanding this claim that democracy is quicker to recognize native worth, every visitor to a democratic society has been struck by its jealous demand for conformity. Such spirit is an outgrowth of competition and suspicion. The democrats well sense that, if they allow people to divide according to abilities and preferences, soon structure will impose itself upon the mass. Hence the adulation of the regular fellow, the political seduction of the common man, and the deep distrust of intellectuals, whose grasp of principle gives them superior insight. This society may even pay tribute to the exemplar of easy morals; for he is the "good fellow," who has about him none of the uncomfortable angularities of the idealist.

It seems plain that the democrats are ignoring a contradiction. Had they the courage to be logical, they would do as their predecessors in ancient Greece and choose their governors by lot. An election, is after all, a highly undemocratic proceeding; the very term means discrimination. How is it possible to choose the best man when by definition there is no best? If a society wishes to be its *natural* self, that is to say, if it wishes to flourish wild, unshaped by anything superior to itself, it should make a perfectly random choice of administrators. Let youth and age, wisdom and folly, courage and cowardice, self-control and dissoluteness, sit together on the bench. This will be representative; this is a cross-section, and there seems no room to question that it would create that society "filled with wonderful variety and disorder" which Plato called democracy.

A footnote, however, must be added to the practice of the Greeks. There were certain officials of highest importance whom they saw fit to choose by election. These were, as might be guessed, the *strategoi*, the military commanders. It was seen that since the very existence of the state depends on them and since a general must have skill, it is better here to take note of differences and admit that in time of emergency authority goes to knowledge. Democratic leadership thus always runs into anomaly. It has been argued that, whatever the aberrations of the democratic state, in periods of crisis such as civil war and the threat of invasion, the people instinctively choose a leader of more than average stature, who will guide them through. Even if this could be proved historically, which is doubtful, it would damage the theoretical foundation of democracy. For it affirms that in time of crisis the people, whether instinctively or otherwise, defer to an elite group who know what to do; when they realize that only direction will save them, they accept it and care not who rails against dictatorship; when a high design becomes imperative, they delegate authority to the extent of placing it beyond their control.[2] In the periods between they are inclined to indulge in the comfort of relaxation and disorder, which is itself a commentary on ideals. Of course, this question is inseparable from that of the end of the state, as that is, in turn, from the end of the individual being.

The writings of the Founding Fathers of the American Union indicate that these political architects approached democracy with a spirit of reservation. Though revolutionaries by historic circumstance, they were capable enough of philosophy to see these dilemmas. The Federalist authors especially were aware that simple majority rule cannot suffice because it does everything without reference; it is an expression of feeling about the moment at the moment, restrained neither by abstract idea nor by precedent. They therefore labored long and with considerable cunning to perfect an instrument which should transcend even the law-making body. This was the Constitution, which in the American system stands for political truth. It is not an unchangeable truth, but the framers placed special obstacles in the way of change. It was hoped that the surmounting of these would prove so laborious and slow that errors would be exposed and the permanently true recognized. In this way they endeavored to protect the populace of a republic against itself. Their action is a rebuke to the romantic theory of human nature, and this will explain why the Constitution has proved so galling to Jacobins. They regard it as a kind of mortmain, and during the administration of Franklin Roosevelt its interpreters were scornfully termed, in an expression indicative of the modern temper, "nine old men."

Edmund Burke was forced to meet the same problem when the French Revolution drove him to examine the foundations of British constitutional liberty. In the absence of a written constitution he had the difficult task of establishing the fact that the English people are bound by a transcending limitation. The long passages in the *Reflections* on succession of the crown has, I think, been misinterpreted; for Burke does not mean, as Thomas Paine asserted, that a single British Parliament made itself a political Adam, by whose enactment all succeeding generations were bound. He rather argues that this act was a precedent in conformity with other precedents, the sum of which binds the English people. If we are to be guided by the experience of the past, there is a perfectly real sense in which precedent is nonrepealable. And precedent was for Burke the principle of continuity and reference. The inheritance of "rational liberty" was thus Britain's protection against subversion.

It has been said countless times in this country that democracy cannot exist without education. The truth concealed in this observation is that only education can be depended on to bring men to see the hierarchy of values. That is another way of saying what has also been affirmed before, that democracy cannot exist without aristocracy. This aristocracy is a leadership which, if it is to endure, must be constantly recruited from democracy; hence it is equally true that aristocracy cannot exist without democracy. But what we have failed to provide against is the corruption of the system of recruitment by equalitarian dogma and the allurements of materialism. There is no difficulty in securing enough agreement for action on the point that education should serve the needs of the people. But all hinges on the interpretation of needs; if the primary need of man is to perfect his spiritual being and prepare for immortality, then education of the mind and the passions will take precedence over all else. The growth of materialism, however, has made this a consideration remote and even incomprehensible to the majority. Those who maintain that education should prepare one for living successfully in this world have won a practically complete victory. Now if it were possible to arrive at a sufficiently philosophical conception of success, there would still remain room for idealistic goals, and attempts have been made to do something like it by defining in philosophical language what constitutes a free man. Yet the prevailing conception is that education must be such as will enable one to acquire enough wealth to live on the plane of the bourgeoisie. That kind of education does not develop the aristocratic virtues. It neither encourages reflection nor inspires a reverence for the good.

In other words, it is precisely because we have lost our grasp of the nature of knowledge that we have nothing to educate with for the salvation of our order. Americans certainly cannot be reproached for failing to invest adequately in the hope that education would prove a redemption. They have built numberless high schools, lavish in equipment, only to see them, under the prevailing scheme of values, turned into social centers and institutions for improving the personality, where teachers, living in fear of constituents, dare not enforce scholarship. They have built colleges on an equal scale, only to see them turned into playgrounds for grown-up children or centers of vocationalism and professionalism. Finally, they have seen pragmatists, as if in peculiar spite against the very idea of hierarchy, endeavoring to turn classes into democratic forums, where the teacher is only a moderator, and no one offends by presuming to speak with superior knowledge.

The formula of popular education has failed democracy because democracy has rebelled at the thought of sacrifice, the sacrifice of time and material goods without which there is no training in intellectual discipline. The spoiled-child psychology, of which I shall say something later, has sought a royal road to learning. In this way, when even its institutions of learning serve primarily the ends of gross animal existence, its last recourse to order is destroyed by appetite.

Every attempt to find a way out of these dilemmas points to a single necessity; some source of authority must be found. The only source of authority whose title is unimpeachable at all times is knowledge. But superiority in knowledge carries prerogative, which implies, of course, distinction and hierarchy. We have seen, too, that the possibility of liberty and the hope of personal improvement rest upon these, for liberty must always work in the name of right reason, which is itself a conception of the scheme of things. The conservatives of our day have a case which only their want of imagination keeps them from making use of in the proposition that levelers are foes of freedom. Where simple massness exists, everyone is in everyone else's way, and a certain perilous liberty has been traded for stultification.

The average man of the present age has a metaphysic in the form of a conception known as "progress." It is certainly to his credit that he does not wish to be a sentimentalist in his endeavors; he wants some measure for purposeful activity; he wants to feel that through the world some increasing purpose runs. And nothing is more common than to hear him discriminate people according to this metaphysic, his term for the less worthy being "unprogressive." But since his metaphysic calls only for magnitude and number, since it is becoming without a goal, it is not a source of distinctions in value. It is a system of quantitative comparison. Its effect therefore has been to collapse the traditional hierarchy and to produce economic man, whose destiny is mere activity.

The mere notion of infinite progress is destructive. If the goal recedes forever, one point is no nearer it than the last. All that we can do is compare meaninglessly yesterday, today, and tomorrow. Aristotle noted that the concept of infinity makes impossible the idea of the good. If a series of things is hierarchically ordered, it is conditioned from top to bottom and so cannot be infinite. If it is infinite, it cannot be conditioned from top to bottom, and there is no higher and lower.

Now such a look at the nature of things is imperative, for our conception of metaphysical reality finally governs our conception of everything else, and, if we feel that creation does not express purpose, it is impossible to find an authorization for purpose in our lives. Indeed, the assertion of purpose in a world we felt to be purposeless would be a form of sentimentality.

3

Fragmentation and Obsession

All ideas are in God, and in so far as they have reference to God, they are true and adequate; and therefore none are inadequate or confused save in so far as they have reference to the individual mind of anyone.

SPINOZA

Whoever argues for a restoration of values is sooner or later met with the objection that one cannot return, or as the phrase is likely to be, "you can't turn the clock back." By thus assuming that we are prisoners of the moment, the objection well reveals the philosophic position of modernism. The believer in truth, on the other hand, is bound to maintain that the things of highest value are not affected by the passage of time; otherwise the very concept of truth becomes impossible. In declaring that we wish to recover lost ideals and values, we are looking toward an ontological realm which is timeless. Only the sheerest relativism insists that passing time renders unattainable one ideal while forcing upon us another. Therefore those that say we can have the integration we wish, and those who say we cannot, differ in their ideas of ultimate reality, for the latter are positing the primacy of time and of matter. And this is the kind of division which prevents us from having one world.

Now the return which the idealists propose is not a voyage backward through time but a return to center, which must be conceived metaphysically or theologically. They are seeking the one which endures and not the many which change and pass, and this search can be only described as looking for the truth. They are making the ancient affirmation that there is a center of things, and they point out that every feature of modern disintegration is a flight from this toward periphery. It is expressible, also, as a movement from unity to individualism. In proportion as man approaches the outer rim, he becomes lost in details, and the more he is preoccupied with details, the less he can understand them. A recovery of certain viewpoints associated with the past would be a recovery of understanding as such, and this, unless we admit ourselves to be helpless in the movement of a deterministic march, is possible at any time. In brief, one does not require a particular standpoint to comprehend the timeless. Let us remember all the while that the very notion of eternal verities is repugnant to the modern temper.

It will be useful to review here this flight toward periphery, or the centrifugal impulse of our culture. In the Middle Ages, when there obtained a comparatively clear perception of reality, the possessor of highest learning was the philosophic doctor. He stood at the center of things because he had mastered principles. On a level far lower were those who had acquired only facts and skills. It was the abandonment of metaphysics and theology which undermined the position of the philosophic doctor, a position remarkably like that prescribed by Plato for the philosopher-king. For the philosophic doctor was in charge of the general synthesis. The assertion that philosophy is queen of studies meant more to him than a figure of speech; knowledge of ultimate matters conferred a right to decide ultimate questions. This is why, for example, the faculty of theology at the Sorbonne could be appealed to on matters of financial operation, which, in our era of fragmentation, would be regarded as exclusively the province of the banker. In the course of the evolution that we have traced the philosophic doctor was displaced; but a substitute had to be found, for synthesis requires the reconciling of all interests.

To take over his task, the dawning modernism chose the gentleman. There was logic in this choice, for the gentleman is a secularized expression of the same thing. Rulers any group must have; and, after repudiating the sanction of religion, the age turned to the product of a training which would approximate religion in breadth and depth. Consequently, there appears at this point a great interest in humanities and liberal arts, in Aristotle's program for the young ruler—Montaigne, Rabelais, Castiglione, Sir Thomas More, Thomas Elyot, and others offered regimens to train men who should be broad enough to deal with the interests of society. Milton's ideal of the educated man, who was ready to perform "all duties, both public and private, of peace and of war," expressed the same thought.

The most important thing about the gentleman was that he was an idealist, though his idealism lacked the deepest foundations. He was bred up to a code of self-restraint which taught resistance to pragmatic temptation. He was definitely a man of sentiment, who refused to put matters on a basis of materialism and self-aggrandizement. One can see this in the convention that the gentleman was a man of his word and in the ritual that he observed toward fallen foes and the weaker. His acceptance of the rules of courtesy militated against egotism. In one thing was he deficient: he had lost sight of the spiritual origin of self-discipline This loss had, of course, grave consequences; yet it cannot be denied that the gentleman can at least partially fill the role of philosophic doctor. He will serve as exemplar to a humanist secularized society as the other did to a religious.

As long as the Western world could maintain a gentleman class, whether by some principle of inheritance or by recruitment from generation to generation, it retained a measure of protection. For it had here a group not wholly absorbed or obsessed, who held a general view of the relationship of things. Though it was somewhat weakened by the difficulty of defining grounds for its authority—the problem of how any man qua man is better than any other—still its presence meant balance, and people had some comfort in the thought that policy was being made by men of "broad views"—for such are the inculcations of liberal education. Gentlemen did not always live up to their ideal, but the existence of an ideal is a matter of supreme importance.

In attenuated form the ideal survives until today, though the forces of modernism conspire to extinguish it. In the countries of Europe, one after another, the gentleman has been ousted by politicians and entrepreneurs, as materialism has given its rewards to the sort of cunning incompatible with any kind of idealism. In the United States the new and the old Europe came into conflict in 1861. The American South not only had cherished the ideal but had given it an infusion of fresh strength, partly through its social organization but largely through its education in rhetoric and law. The South's tradition of learning was the Ciceronian tradition of eloquent wisdom, and this circumstance explains why the major creative political figures of America, from Jefferson through Lincoln to Wilson, have come from this section. But the Civil War brought defeat to Ciceronian humanism, and thereafter the South turned to commerce and technology in its economic life and to the dialectic of New England and of Germany in its educational endeavors. The gentleman was left to walk the stage an impecunious eccentric, protected by a certain sentimentality but no longer understood. Europe, after the agony of the first World War, turned to the opposite type for leadership, to gangsters, who, though they are often good entrepreneurs, are without codes and without inhibitions.[1] Such leaders in Europe have given us a preview of what the collapse of values and the reign of specialization will produce.

By far the most significant phase of the theory of the gentleman is its distrust of specialization. It is an ancient belief, going back to classical antiquity, that specialization of any kind is illiberal in a freeman. A man willing to bury himself in the details of some

small endeavor has been considered lost to these larger considerations which must occupy the mind of the ruler. The attitude is
well expressed in King Philip's famous taunt to his son Alexander,
who had learned to perform skilfully upon the flute: "Are you not
ashamed, son, to play so well?" It is contained in the hierarchy of
knowledge in Aristotle's *Metaphysics*. It is explained by Plutarch
with the observation that "he who busies himself with mean oc-
cupations produces in the very pains he takes about things of little
use evidence against himself of his negligence and indisposition to
what is really good." The attitude is encountered in men of letters
of the seventeenth and eighteenth centuries. They wished to be
known as gentlemen first and as writers only incidentally. Finally,
there is the story of the barber who congratulated Napoleon for
not having a scholar's knowledge of the proper pronunciation of
Alexandria. To regard these as exhibitions of priggishness is to
miss the point entirely; they are expressions of contempt for the
degradation of specialization and pedantry. Specialization develops only part of a man; a man partially developed is deformed; and
one deformed is the last person to be thought of as a ruler; so runs
the irresistible logic of the position.

Science is therefore not a pursuit for such a one. Because it
demands an ever more minute inspection of the physical world, it
makes an ideal of specialism, and one may recall Nietzsche's figure
of the scientist who spends his life studying the brain structure of
the leech. Is it necessary to press further the point that, when such
matters come to be pursued as knowledge, the task of synthesis
approaches impossibility?

The position of the philosophic doctor and of his secular heir,
the gentleman, was thus correct. For them the highest knowledge
concerned, respectively, the relation of men to God and the relation of men to men. They did not expect to learn what they most
needed to know by fleeing center, that is, by diving ever deeper
into the mysteries of the physical world. Such is escape and moral
defeatism. When Socrates declared in the *Phaedrus* that he learned

not from the trees of the country but from the men of the city, he was exposing the fallacy of scientism.

At this point the student ceases to be doctor of philosophy since he is no longer capable of philosophy. He has made himself an essentially ridiculous figure, and this would have been perceived had not the public, undergoing the same process of debasement, found a different ground on which to venerate him. Knowledge *was* power. The very character of the new researches lent them to *ad hoc* purposes. It was soon a banality that the scholar contributes to civilization by adding to its dominion over nature. It is just as if Plato's philosopher had left the city to look at the trees and then had abandoned speculative wisdom for dendrology. The people who would urge just this course are legion among us today. The facts on the periphery, they feel, are somehow more certain.

The modern knower may be compared to an inebriate who, as he senses his loss of balance, endeavors to save himself by fixing tenaciously upon certain details and thus affords the familiar exhibition of positiveness and arbitrariness. With the world around him beginning to heave, he grasps at something that will come within a limited perception. So the scientist, having lost hold upon organic reality, clings the more firmly to his discovered facts, hoping that salvation lies in what can be objectively verified.

From this comes a most important symptom of our condition, the astonishing vogue of factual information. It is naturally impossible for anyone to get along without some knowledge that he feels can be relied on. Having been told by the relativists that he cannot have truth, he now has "facts." One notes that even in everyday speech the word *fact* has taken the place of *truth*; "it is a fact" is now the formula for a categorical assertion. Where fact is made the criterion, knowledge has been rendered unattainable. And the public is being taught systematically to make this fatal confusion of factual particulars with wisdom. On the radio and in magazines and newspapers appear countless games and quizzes designed to test one's stock of facts. The acquisition of unrelated details becomes an end in itself and takes the place of the true ideal of education. So misleading is the program that one widely circulated column invites readers to test their "horse sense" by answering the factual queries it propounds. The same attention to peripheral matter long ago invaded the schools, at the topmost levels, it must be confessed, where it made nonsense of literary study and almost ruined history. The supposition that facts will speak for themselves is of course another abdication of intellect. Like impressionist artists, the objectivists prostrate themselves before exterior reality on the assumption that the organizing work of the mind is deceptive.

Plato reminded us that at any stage of an inquiry it is important to realize whether we are moving toward, or away from, first principles. The significance of the movement we are here tracing is that the former distrust of specialization has been supplanted by its opposite, a distrust of generalization. Not only has man become a specialist in practice, he is being taught that special facts represent the highest form of knowledge. Mathematical logic, with its attempt to evade universal classification, is an excellent example of the tendency. The extreme of nominalism appears when men fear, as many do today, to make even those general groupings which are requisite to ordinary activities. We are developing a phobia toward simple predication. Sensing that even expository statement is a form of argument and that argument implies the existence of truth, we shrink back by clinging to our affirmation of particulars. They seem innocuous. Any extension beyond, toward center, may involve grave duties.

Since liberalism became a kind of official party line, we have been enjoined against saying things about races, religions, or national groups, for, after all, there is no categorical statement without its implication of value, and values begin divisions among men. We must not define, subsume, or judge; we must rather rest on the periphery and display "sensibility toward the cultural expression of all lands and peoples." This is a process of emasculation.

It should be plain from the foregoing that modern man is suffering from a severe fragmentation of his world picture. This fragmentation leads directly to an obsession with isolated parts. Obsession, according to the canons of psychology, occurs when an innocuous idea is substituted for a painful one. The victim simply avoids recognizing the thing which will hurt. We have seen that the most painful confession for the modern egotist to make is that there is a center of responsibility. He has escaped it by taking his direction with reference to the smallest points. The theory of empiricism is plausible because it assumes that accuracy about small matters prepares the way for valid judgment about large ones. What happens, however, is that the judgments are never made. The pedantic empiricist, buried in his little province of phenomena, imagines that fidelity to it exempts him from concern with larger aspects of reality—in the case of science, from consideration of whether there is reality other than matter.

Such obsession with fragments has grave consequences for the individual psychology, not the least of which is fanaticism. Now fanaticism has been properly described as redoubling one's effort after one's aim has been forgotten, and this definition will serve as a good introduction to the fallacy of technology, which is the conclusion that because a thing can be done, it must be done. The means absorb completely, and man becomes blind to the very concept of ends; indeed, even among those who make an effort at reflection, an idea grows that ends must wait upon the discovery of means. Hence proceeds a fanatical interest in the properties of matter which is psychopathic because it involves escape, substitution, and the undercurrent of anxiety which comes of knowing that the real issue has not been met.

If, then, the substitution of means for ends is the essence of fanaticism, we can better recognize the peril in which science and technology have placed our souls. Sanity is a proportion with reference to purpose; there is no standard of sanity when the whole question of ends is omitted. The obsession, however, is a source of great comfort to the obsessed. It is a reprieve from the real ordeal. Let us not question the genuineness of the sigh of relief when people are allowed to go back to their test tubes and their facts.

A high degree of instability is another aspect of this psychopathology. It is not to be anticipated that rational self-control will flourish in the presence of fixation upon parts. Workers confined to very small tasks have been found to show a special tendency toward emotional instability, and one sees everywhere in urban populations a volatility of temperament that contrasts with the steadiness of the man living close to nature. It shows itself in fits of fickle admiration, in excitation over slight causes, in hypersuggestibility and proneness to panic, all of which render most unlikely that sober estimate of men and things characterizing the philosopher. An observer coming into some modern metropolis from a province where traditional values are yet rooted is impressed by the way in which judgments are made without reference. He encounters arguments which are brilliant, perhaps, within a narrow scope, but which, when pushed a step in the direction of first principles, collapse for want of basic relevance. He finds movements, propagated with all the cleverness of sophisticated techniques, which appear absurd as soon as their presuppositions about human nature and human destiny are laid bare. The fragmentary character of such thinking permits contradictions and sudden reversals, and these prevent emotional composure in the face of choice.

We have now observed some of the results of the evolution from philosophic doctor to gentleman to specialist. At this point we find that the specialist is inferior psychically to his predecessors. He is like some parvenu striving to cover up with self-assertion the guilty feeling that he is not qualified. For the truth is that fanaticism and emotional instability, tension and flightiness, are incompatible with that seasoned maturity which we expect in a leader. The man who understands has reason to be sure of himself; he has the repose of mastery. He is the sane man, who carries his center of gravity in himself; he has not succumbed to obsession which binds him to a fragment of reality. People tend to trust the judgments of an integrated personality and will prefer them even to the official opinions of experts. They rightly suspect that *expertise* conceals some abnormality of viewpoint. Thus the specialist stands ever at the borderline of psychosis. It has been remarked that when one passes among the patients of a psychopathic ward, he encounters among the several sufferers every aspect of normal personality in morbid exaggeration, so that it would be possible theoretically to put together a supermind by borrowing something from each. And as one passes through modern centers of enterprise and of higher learning, he is met with similar autonomies of development. Each would be admired for his little achievement of power and virtuosity; each is resentful of subordination because, for him, a specialty has become the world. The public, retaining a certain perspective by virtue of its naïve realism, calls them "lopsided." There is no reason to quarrel with the metaphor. The scientist, the technician, the scholar, who have left the One for the Many are puffed up with vanity over their ability to describe precisely some minute portion of the world. Men so obsessed with fragments can no more be reasoned with than other psychotics, and hence the observation of Ortega y Gasset that the mere task of saving our civilization demands "incalculably subtle powers." Civilization must be saved from some who profess to be its chief lights and glories.

Thoughtful people today are sometimes moved to wonder why the world no longer has use for a liberally educated class. Surely the answer lies in this abandonment of generalization for specialization, which is the very process of fragmentation. The world has wilfully narrowed responsibility. Now the question of whether it is possible for everyone to be a philosopher, if we are willing to go back to essentials, is a part of the larger question of whether everyone can participate in the aristocratic virtues. This is the problem of wisdom and self-control, and there have existed societies in which a far larger proportion of the people had access to general responsibility, which acted as a counterpoise to these psychopathic tendencies. Let us look, for example, at preindustrial America. The feature of that society which contrasts most strongly with our own was the distribution of centers of influence and authority. We might take as a single instance a Vermont farmer of the 1850's, certainly not one to give himself airs, yet a vessel of some responsibility and, to that extent, an aristocrat by calling. He has been properly admired for his independence, by which is meant not isolation from community life—on the contrary, he appears to have been active in town meeting and at the poll—but opportunity and disposition to decide for himself according to a rational and enduring code of values. His acres may have been rocky, but he appraised his situation and assumed direction. He rose early because the relationship between effort and reward was clear to him. There was a rhythm to his task which humanized it, each day bringing a certain round of duties, and the seasons themselves imposing a larger pattern, as when haying time arrived. At the end of a day he might remain up until nine o'clock with the weekly newspaper, not flipping through comics and sporting news but reading its political disquisitions to weigh and consider as carefully as Bacon could have desired. He observed the Fourth of July, Thanksgiving, and Christmas with some recollection of what they signified. He remained poor, but he was not unmanned; he had enough character to say No.

With the advance of industrialism this type of individual is exploited and then, because he is exploited, contemned. Native dignity becomes an old fashion, and character is often an obstruction to the wheels of economic progress. Indeed, the sort of social hierarchy we have described as reflecting knowledge of value is abolished, and there is substituted a structure consisting of a mass of workers below and a small group of elite, who are themselves technicians, at the top. The workers are likely not to know what they are producing, and the managers are likely not to care. Division of labor may become so minute that it is impossible for the individual to grasp the ethical implications of his task, even if he were disposed to try. And when we harness this industrial organization to modern political bureaucracy, we get a monster of frightful aspect. Under such arrangement the state not only unmans its citizens but makes criminals of them in addition.

There could be no better example of this than the atomic-bomb project of the United States in the second World War. At Oak Ridge, Tennessee, a force of seventy thousand persons labored at an undertaking whose nature they knew little or nothing about; in fact, wartime propaganda had been so effective that they took pride in their ignorance and boasted of it as a badge of honor or as a sign of co-operation—in what? It is just possible that a few, and I should be willing to say a very few, had they known that their efforts were being directed to the slaughter of noncombatants on a scale never before contemplated, or to a perfection of brutality as we have defined the term, might have refused complicity. Perhaps they would have had some concept of war as an institution which forbids aimless killing; perhaps they would have had a secret feeling that the world is morally designed and that offenses of this kind, under whatever auspices committed, bring retribution; in any case, it is just possible that a few of these anonymous toilers would have given a thought to the larger responsibility. It was rumored that among the world's elite concerned with atomic research there were a few who declined to participate in an operation so contrary to the canons of civilization. Their names have remained unsung. It is to their credit that they rose above specialization, but to do this they had to contemplate ends. The laborers in the vast enterprise were in no such position, but few tears have been shed for them. Imagine the modern state considering a referendum to conscience! The bomb was an unparalleled means; was this not enough? Just so does modern industrial and political organization, which is irrational hierarchy, make the citizen an ethical eunuch. If Thoreau felt, in his time, that it was a disgrace even to be associated with the government, what would he have felt in this? These corrupt bureaucracies are contemptuous of the people, in whose name they so piously speak.

Thus atomic energy, the final discovery of Prometheus, should compel all to see the imperative nature of the question of who shall control. It is, of course, a question that should have been asked long ago about the potential represented by machinery. And our conception of the problem seems to be yet in an extremely elementary stage, for we are arguing whether one nation, or a group of nations, or a federation of all nations should be custodian. Eventually the question of who within the group, national or international, can be trusted with such means will have to be faced. The conclusion, so vexatious to democracy, that wisdom and not popularity qualifies for rule may be forced upon us by the peril in atomic energy. Wisdom does not lie on the periphery.

Granting that the bomb project was an extreme case, though it may be the typical case of the future, we can discern elsewhere the steady trend toward fragmentation and irresponsibility. As a system of production becomes "functionally rationalized," the worker is made to surrender both freedom and initiative. As long as the political order remains stable, he may maintain a robot-like existence. But when it breaks down and he is thrown back upon his own resources, it becomes apparent that these resources have been allowed to diminish. Unaccustomed to determining anything about the purpose and the relationships of his work, he cannot even think in terms large enough to embrace the total situation. The enforced irresponsibility has itself become a factor in pathology, for a burden of responsibility is, after all, the best means of getting anyone to think straight. If he is made to feel that he is accountable for results, he looks steadily at the situation and endeavors to discover what is really true in it. This is a discipline. But when he has long been absolved of the duty of thinking, he may be seized with a sense of helplessness and panic when the necessity of it is thrust upon him. In such circumstances it is quite natural for him to turn to some member of the managerial elite, who in the industrial age of society is himself a specialist.

By losing sight of what the good life demands, he has allowed himself to be maneuvered into a position in which he is not permitted to be a whole man. There is every indication that he retains the same capacity for loyalty, but what has he to be loyal to? The highly unstable character of our political world must be ascribed at least in part to repressions. If tidal waves of feeling move beneath the surface and find no outlet save in obsession, we cannot be surprised at monstrous perversions. The separation which the German was able to make between his fragment of a technology and the political program into which he poured his feeling offers a clue to much. Visitors to Germany after the collapse of the Third Reich reported hearing scientists say, "What have I to do with politics? I am a technician." It is impossible that such people should feel a sense of guilt. To give these or any modern people a sense of guilt, it would be necessary to go back and explain the sin of Prometheus. Similar pleas no doubt would have been made by the toilers at Oak Ridge had the decision gone against their side. The fact that as the war went on the Germans put more and more faith in technology, launching rocket bombs at a time when they could serve no purpose but the creation of a spirit of vengeance, illustrates how blind to total reality one may become through absorption in means.

We have confined ourselves thus far to the kind of obsession which results from attention to peripheral matter and to specialization of labor, but there is another way in which science and its metaphysical handmaiden, progress, discourage sanity. This is its exaltation of "becoming" over "being." In effect, the domination of becoming produces another sort of fragmentation, which may be called "presentism." Allen Tate has made the point that many modern people to whom the word "provincial" is anathema are themselves provincials in time to an extreme degree. Indeed, modernism is in essence a provincialism, since it declines to look beyond the horizon of the moment, just as the countryman may view with suspicion whatever lies beyond his county. There is a strong reason to group this with psychopathic phenomena because it involves impairment of memory, which is known to be one of the commonest accompaniments of mental pathology. It is apparent, moreover, that those who are in rebellion against memory are the ones who wish to live without knowledge; and we can, in fact, tell from their conduct that they act more than others on instinct and sensation. A frank facing of the past is unpleasant to the tenderminded, teaching as it does sharp lessons of limitation and retribution. Yet, the painful lessons we would like to forget are precisely the ones which should be kept for reference. Santayana has reminded us that those who cannot remember the past are condemned to repeat it, and not without reason did Plato declare that a philosopher must have a good memory.

An interesting commentary on presentism is that people close to the soil appear to have longer memories than have the urban masses. Traditions there live for generations; what their grandfathers did is real to them. Consequently they may be said to assimilate lessons. The provincial in time sees that interpretation of the past requires reflection and generalization, which take him beyond the moment. He clutches at the temporal fragment. More fundamentally, he is opposing timelessness, though the timeless cannot be permanently obscured or evaded; it keeps up with us like a monitory shadow. The very possibility that there may exist timeless truths is a reproach to the life of laxness and indifference which modern egotism encourages. It is entirely likely, therefore, that concentration upon the moment is another outlet through obsession.

In this way ideas which have their reference to the periphery or the *individuum*, to the particular in space and time, are false and stand in the way of integration. But to those who believe in transcendentals, progress is without relation to time and space. It is possible, therefore, to think of a metaphysical course toward center, which will be neither a going-backward nor a going-forward in the current sense of these phrases. After such thinking we find ourselves looking upon the specialist as a man possessed of an evil spirit. Next we might find ourselves admiring the internal aplomb of the gentleman, though this would be but another stage of the way. And then, as we begin to inquire what makes the gentleman, we should soon be looking in the direction of the philosophic doctor for a yet profounder integration of character. To Philistines and apostles of the Whig theory of history, this would be retrogression, and we will agree that it calls for sacrifice of many things they regard as indispensable. Like peace, regeneration carries a price which those who think of it idly will balk at. But I propose to tell this part of the story in the last three chapters.

4

Egotism in Work and Art

All persons chronically diseased are egotists, whether the disease be
of the mind or the body; whether it be sin, sorrow, or merely the
more tolerable calamity of some endless pain, or mischief among the
cords of mortal life. Such individuals are made acutely conscious of
self, by the torture in which it dwells. Self, therefore, grows to be
so prominent an object with them that they cannot but present it to
the face of every casual passer-by.

HAWTHORNE

As One views modern man in his innumerable exhibitions of irresponsibility and defiance, one may discern, if he has the courage to see what he sees—which, as Charles Péguy reminded us, is
the higher courage—a prodigious egotism. This egotism, which
is another form of fragmentation, is a consequence of that fatal
decision to make a separate self the measure of value. A figure
from Neo-Platonism is suggested, and one may picture the original
spirit manifesting itself in many particulars, which lose sight of
their original source and decide to set up godheads in their own
right. Since under conditions of modern freedom the individual
thinks only of his rights, he does not refer his action to the external
frame of obligation. His wish is enough. He cannot be disciplined
on the theoretical level, and on the practical level he is disciplined

only by some hypostatized social whole whose methods become brutal as its authority turns out to be, on investigation, merely human. The sin of egotism always takes the form of withdrawal. When personal advantage becomes paramount, the individual passes out of the community. We do not mean the state, with its apparatus of coercion, but the spiritual community, where men are related on the plane of sentiment and sympathy and where, conscious of their oneness, they maintain a unity not always commensurable with their external unification.

Such withdrawal, which has been given the disarming name of enlightened selfishness and which more often than not is inspired by the desire to be "equal," is pulverizing modern society. And there is no precept in modern ideology with which to rebuke it; for, is not this equal man a kind of king, superior to the trappings of royalty, and cannot such a one do what he will with his life? The various declarations of independence have given him freedom from all the bondages. Yet the blight which has fallen today on all sorts of human relationship must be ascribed to this psychological and even physical withdrawal from sympathy.

Inevitably there follows an increase of selfishness. It is the simple nature of egotism to view things out of proportion, the "I" becoming dominant and the entire world suffering a distortion. Once more we are face to face with the fact of alienation from reality. No man who knows himself in his *ab extra* relationships can be egotistic. But he who is cognizant mainly of self suffers an actual derangement; as Plato saw: "the excessive love of self is in reality the source to each man of all offenses; for the lover is blinded about the beloved, so that he judges wrongly of the just, the good, and the honorable, and thinks that he ought always prefer his own interest to the truth."

Accordingly, self-absorption is a process of cutting one's self off from the "real" reality and therefore from social harmony. I think it is worth noting, too, that Nathaniel Hawthorne, an earnest student of erring souls, concluded, after a lifetime of introspection and reflection, that egotism is the unpardonable sin. He exposed through allegory what "social-mindedness" endeavors to combat in contemporary society. Its causes must now be described.

The split in the theory of knowledge which took place at the time of the Renaissance is enough to account for that form of ignorance which is egotism. Under the world view possessed by medieval scholars, the path of learning was a path to self-depreciation, and the *philosophiae doctor* was one who had at length seen a rational ground for *humilitas*. Study and meditation led him to a proper perspective on self, which then, instead of caricaturing the world with the urgency of its existence and the vehemence of its desires, found a place in the hierarchy of reality. Dante's *In la sua voluntade è nostra pace* is the final discovery. Thus knowledge for the medieval idealist prepared the way for self-effacement.

An opposing conception comes in with Bacon's "knowledge is power." If the aim of knowledge is domination, it is hardly to be supposed that the possessors of knowledge will be indifferent to their importance. On the contrary, they begin to swell; they seek triumphs in the material world (knowledge being meanwhile necessarily degraded to skills) which inflate their egotism and self-consideration. Such is a brief history of how knowledge passes from a means of spiritual redemption to a basis for intellectual pride.

In Greek fable, as in Christian, it is asserted that there is a forbidden knowledge which brings nothing into the world but woe. Our generation has had ample demonstration of what that knowledge is. It is knowledge of the useful rather than of the true and the good, of techniques rather than of ends. If we insist that our problems are philosophical, we cannot expect a return to selflessness without an epistemological revision which will elevate the study of essences above that of particulars and so put in their proper modest place those skills needed to manipulate the world. Nothing can be done until we have decided whether we are primarily interested in truth.

In the absence of truth there is no necessity, and this observation may serve as an index to the position of the modern egotist. Having become incapable of knowing, he becomes incapable of working, in the sense that all work is a bringing of the ideal from potentiality into actuality. We perceive this simply when his egotism prevents realization that he is an obligated creature, bound to rational employment. The modern worker does not, save in rare instances, respond to the ideal in the task.

Before the age of adulteration it was held that behind each work there stood some conception of its perfect execution. It was this that gave zest to labor and served to measure the degree of success. To the extent that the concept obtained, there was a teleology in work, since the laborer toiled not merely to win sustenance but to see this ideal embodied in his creation. Pride in craftsmanship is well explained by saying that to labor is to pray, for conscientious effort to realize an ideal is a kind of fidelity. The craftsman of old did not hurry, because the perfect takes no account of time and shoddy work is a reproach to character. But character itself is an expression of self-control, which does not come of taking the easiest way. Where character forbids self-indulgence, transcendence still hovers around.

When utilitarianism becomes enthroned and the worker is taught that work is use and not worship, interest in quality begins to decline. How many times have we heard exclamations of wonder at the care which went into some article of ancient craftsmanship before modern organization drove a wedge between the worker and his product! There is the difference between expressing one's self in form and producing quantity for a market with an eye to speculation. Péguy wished to know what had become of the honor of work. It has succumbed to the same forces as have all other expressions of honor.

It is a normal thing for any class to adopt the ideas of a class above it (and here is another argument for the importance of *rational* hierarchy), even when those ideas happen to be about itself. That series of subversive events which raised the middle class to a position of dominance allowed it not only to prescribe the conditions of labor but also to frame the world of discourse of economics. Here begins modern labor's history; in conflict with an exploiting and irresponsible bourgeoisie, it found no alternative but to avail itself of the bourgeois philosophy and strike back.

Accordingly, workers' organizations accepted in their practice the idea that labor is a commodity when they began the capitalist technique of restricting production in the interest of price. Labor which is bought and sold by anonymous traders cannot feel a consecration to task. Its interest becomes that of commercialism generally: how much can be had for how little? Today workers seek to diminish their commodity in order to receive a larger return within the price framework. Controlled and artificial scarcity becomes a means of class promotion, or even of class survival. Thorstein Veblen saw financiers restricting the production which engineers were eager to realize; now we see, in addition, labor organizations restricting output in the interest of group advantage.

The object is not to say that labor is more or less to blame than other groups of society; it is rather to show that when egotism becomes dominant and men are applauded for looking to their own interest first, statesmanship and philosophy must leave the picture. The evidence shows that the middle classes spread the infection. However that may be, the consequence is a fragmentation of society which cannot stop short of complete chaos.

When the egotist thinks of himself first and the task second, he is, like the ontologist mentioned at the beginning, denying the reality of forms imperfectly realized. The reality then is merely the actuality which his desire or whim cares to produce. He thinks not of subordinating self to end but of subordinating end to self. Such reversal of role makes rational distribution impossible, for only when labor is seen in the context of its performance can a rational estimate of reward be made. We know how to reward the carpenter qua carpenter; we do not know how to reward the egotist who comes with assertions of how much he is worth. That payment to labor which merely reflects the outcome of a tug of war is removed from philosophical determination.

In this way disintegration has placed labor in a position in which it must compete against other groups in a manner which cannot bring ultimate advantage to any of those involved. What we get at length is the institutionalization of the unilateral settlement. Every group is given freedom and even inducement to help itself at the expense of other groups, and it has been found that the most effective means is simple extortion—a withdrawal from communal effort until self-inspired demands are met. This is, of course, the egocentric solution. The bourgeoisie first betrayed society through capitalism and finance, and now labor betrays it by embracing a scheme of things which sees profit only, not duty and honor, in work. This view will seem hopelessly unrealistic to those who do not admit that sentiment toward the whole is the only ultimate means of measuring value. Yet it will eventually appear that the greatest disservice done to our age—and it has been done by sentimental humanitarianism—was this denial of necessary connection between effort and reward. The reign of sophists, economists, and calculators has ushered in the era of egotistic competition, which makes sabotage an approved instrumentality. The laborer feels justified in putting a stop to the whole productive process if his own appraisal of his service is not accepted; and this appraisal is not made with reference to what society exists for—this, we repeat, is a matter for enlightened sentiment—but with reference to his own gratification.

It would be an unpopular man who should suggest to the present generation that work is a divine ordinance. The idea has been grouped with the widely misinterpreted divine right of kings, and, if we examine the matter closely, we find that the two are indeed related. For whether one is a worker or a ruler, the question becomes at once: What is the real source of his authority to act? That Governor John Winthrop found a solution for this problem is worth knowing. In a statement to the General Court of Massachusetts in 1645 he said: "The questions that have troubled the country have been about the authority of the magistracy, and the liberty of the people. It is you who have called us unto this office; but being called, we have our authority from God; it is the ordinance of God, and it hath the image of God stamped upon it; and the contempt of it has been vindicated by God with terrible examples of his vengeance." In other words, the leader may be chosen by the people, but he is guided by the right; and, in the same way, we may say that the worker may be employed by anyone, but that he is directed by the autonomous ideal in the task.

Now when men cease to believe that labor is a divine ordinance, their attitude toward it becomes like their attitude toward the secularized state. The state is then wholly man's contrivance; but egotistic men are competitors—they are seeking to get the better of one another and to evade demands made on them by their theoretical equals. Much of the effort of modern politicians is devoted to convincing us that men serve best when they are serving one another. But the one consideration which would make this true is left out; service to others is the best service when the effort of all is subsumed under a transcendental conception. Material gratification does not provide this, and here one has the reason why a secularized state finally breeds an intense hatred of politicians, who are trying to get men to accept one another as taskmasters. Work is not to be performed "as ever in my great Taskmaster's eye," but for my neighbor, whom I despise.

The situation deteriorates because the idea that work is something apportioned out by men leaves people discontent with their portion and dubious about whether work is a good thing at all. How technology reinforces the latter feeling will be discussed later; it is sufficient to note here that the ancient moral injunction to labor fades when we regard our work as cut out for us by men, who, by present dogma, are no better than ourselves. That curious modern hypostatization "service" is often called in to substitute for the now incomprehensible doctrine of vocation. It tries to secure subordination by hypothezising something larger than self, which turns out, however, to be only a multitude of selfish selves. The familiar change from quality to quantity may again be noted; one serves not the higher part of the self (this entails hierarchy too, pointing finally to commission from above) but merely consumer demand. And who admires those at the top of a hierarchy of consumption? Man as consuming animal is thus seen to be not enough.

Like other theories of individualism and materialism, the right of man to be an egotist finds support in various plausibilities. Is not man the first thing to be considered? it will be asked. Is he not to be given preference over abstract rights, privileges, and so forth? What this question fails to see is that man's egotism renders impossible that kind of organization which would allow him to prosper to a degree. When he puts himself first in this sense, the victory is Pyrrhic. The only way to give him anything that will last is to place him in a structure where opportunity and ability may meet. This cannot be done by considering egotistic demands first; such shortsightedness destroys the supporting structure. Thus sentimental humanitarianism, ignorant of fundamental realities but ever attentive to desires, wrecks society.

The egotism of work increasingly poses the problem of what source will procure sufficient discipline to hold men to production. When each becomes his own taskmaster and regards work as a curse which he endures only to gain means of subsistence, will he not constantly seek to avoid it? An employer was recently heard to remark that we have plenty of persons today who can tell us why a machine will not work but none will tell us why men will not work. The new socialist governments of Europe, finding production falling off, have already begun to use the incentive of piecework. Elsewhere open use has been made of war and the fear of war to hold workers to their jobs; and President Truman's proposal on a certain occasion to confront recalcitrant labor with military induction is the clearest proof that a nation which egotism has paralyzed will, in an emergency, have recourse to its most rigorous form of discipline, the services trained for armed combat. It thus appears that the spirit of self, which has made the worker lose sight of the calling of his task and to think only of aggrandizement, is the plainest invitation yet offered by the Western world to the tyranny of force.

Such, then, are the consequences when egotism begins to influence that daily service which is labor. But there is a yet more sensitive register of this influence in that specialized activity known as art, and here the testimony is as concurrent as it is overwhelming. It is illuminating to trace the ravages of egotism in aesthetic expression.

There is a significant saying that nature imitates art, and it is often pointed out that in the great epochs of expression nature and art seem faithful to one another, so that what art creates does not fade. But what are we to say of epochs like our own in which art appears unnatural, grotesque, and irresponsible, so that we feel it to be the product of some dangerous subjectivism? Is not this the parting of the ways which occurs when man leaves the truth of reality and expresses himself in isolation? Nature does not follow where art becomes not truer than history, not ideally true, but false to the higher reality.

It is egotism which enforces the separation between nature—by which is meant here the enduring reality—and art.

A historical survey of this aspect of the descent may well begin with a glance at literature. The great changes affecting the literature of our time began with those subterranean forces which erupted in the French Revolution. Though much of the eighteenth century was a period of competing tendencies, it was the romantic revolt which finally carried the day. This revolt would seem to have made its first appearance in the doctrine of ethical optimism propounded by the Earl of Shaftesbury. In opposition to the orthodox view of human nature, which acknowledged original sin and preached the necessity of education and restraint, it taught that man has a natural moral sense which can be relied on not only to recognize virtue but to delight in it. The important consequence for literature was the sanctioning of impulse, which now became the subject of endless and varied exploitation.

The first proof that this was to be a serious influence on literature emerged with the poetry and fiction of sensibility. Poets such as Joseph Wharton, William Collins, Edward Young, and, later, Oliver Goldsmith, professing a contempt for the formal life of cities and the conventions of prevailing literary fashion, uncovered their senses, so to speak, to the beauty and strangeness of nature and talked of the simple occurrences of life. Then followed the novelist of sensibility—Thomas Amory, Laurence Sterne, and others—who put their heroes through a sort of sentimental vagabondage and held them up to admiration as men of feeling. Sterne's remark that the pen governed him and not he it is a revealing commentary upon the mood of revolt against intellect.

Implied in the premises which Shaftesbury set forth was sentimental comedy. Previously comedy had been satirical, and satire, it is important to note, always bespeaks an age which recognizes good and evil and makes distinctions among human beings accordingly. In a world where all men are naturally good, the erring one is merely misled; confront him with the consequence of his ways and he reforms, as did the hero in the sentimental comedy.

These ideas together imply that man is good, that experience is good, and that therefore the career of any individual may be worth following in the fulness of its unique detail. When Rousseau wrote at the beginning of the *Confessions*: "I am different from all men I have seen. If I am not better, at least I am different," he expressed directly the note of egotistic sensibility.

The Romantic deluge followed at the beginning of the nine-

teenth century. There appeared at this point a group of great ex-
pressionists, men of resourcefulness and enormous activity, whose
influence on literature has been second, perhaps, only to that of
the Elizabethans. They sounded with greater insistence the ideas of
the pre-Romantics which we have just reviewed. Foremost was the
impulse of revolt against conventions and institutions. Whether it
was Wordsworth cultivating the speech of ordinary men and endeavoring to read "the common face of nature," or Byron declaim-
ing upon the ruins of Rome, or Shelley denouncing "bloody faith,
the foulest birth of time," a theme of emancipation from the sentiments and forms which had brought in European culture persists.

This motif was likely to be accompanied by intensive explo-
rations of the individual consciousness, with self-laceration and
self-pity. The sensitive individual turned inward and there discovered an appalling well of melancholy and unhappiness, which was
attributed to the perverse circumstances of the world. Thus we
behold in spectacular form the new familiar act of withdrawal as
the individual fosters self-awareness. The young romantic Goethe
in *Werther*, and Shelley crying, "I fall upon the thorns of life, I
bleed," continue the indulgence in egocentric sensibility.

During the whole of the century this flood rushed on, but it later
assumed expressions which are to be grasped, it seems, only upon
the level of complex significance. Some of the Romantics, despite
the delight in disorder dictated by Romanticism, turned into the
most meticulous craftsmen in literary history. This anomalous development was owing to a realization by the more perceptive that
raw experience, exaggerated sensibility, and large moral and political enthusiasms alone mean artistic bankruptcy. Some therefore
sought in form a means of salvation, but it was with a Romantic's
interest in form. The French have a phrase which seems to describe
this exactly. It was a *maladie du scrupule* which drove Flaubert
and the De Goncourts and, later, Henry James and numerous poets to suppose that unremitting attention to form would save the

subject matter of Romantic art. Hence we have prodigies of faithful observation, *le mot juste*, and a fineness of texture in poetry; but somehow another fragmentation has taken place. Form has become obsessive. Confinement to form is one means of evading those heavier responsibilities which must be related to one's total awareness or his view of man's destiny.

Concurrent with this attempt to escape bankruptcy through brilliance of form was another which sought to escape it through imagination. In one respect, the Romanticists who became Symbolists were not faithful to the premises of the movement; in another, they were conspicuously faithful. Symbolism is a reaction against the deification of the material world, because the symbol is always a sign of things that are not compresent in time and space. The symbol by its nature transcends and thus points to the world beyond the world. So the Symbolists were reaching for the outer reality, which to the simple early Romantics was but a vague presence. They found that experience did not interpret itself, and they were driven to difficult feats of intellection and representation in their effort to convey the significant reality.

But the Symbolists retained a Romantic's interest in the intimate and in the individual, with the result that their symbols came not from some ideology universally accepted but from experiences almost private. Possibly the libertarian mood survives here: the artist still wishes to have free range and to soar, and a normal medium of communication would hold him too close to the social context. We must certainly acknowledge that it was the vulgarization of language through journalism and kindred activities which impelled many literary artists, including some workers in prose, to seek out fresh media. One may honor them for their heroism, even though the result was not from all points of view fortunate. At any rate, writers increasingly employed the fleeting metaphor and the faintly evocative symbol. And, while it is unjust to talk, as some have, of "the cult of unintelligibility" and of "poets talking to themselves," it seems fair to say that the Symbolists put themselves under very special handicaps and limitations, which grievously widened the gap between poetry and the public.

Let us now turn to the story of music, a medium which, as Schopenhauer observed, is uniquely related to the will. Here we discover a decline which extends from the fugues of Bach to the cacophonous arrangements of modern jazz.

The degenerative influences upon music parallel closely those upon literature, with the difference of a slight time lag. The eighteenth century remained a strongly classical period wherein music expressed the aristocratic and international qualities of the social order. Mozart, its most perfect exponent, accepted "without a suspicion of discomfort" the traditional forms, furnishing an example of freedom and restraint, of balance and resiliency. Here is one of the happiest illustrations, occurring just prior to the Romantic deluge, of what is possible with freedom and law. The portents of change came with Beethoven, whose sympathy with the French Revolution must not be overlooked. A great architect in music, Beethoven, nevertheless, through the introduction of dynamism and of strains of individualism pointed the way which the succeeding century was to take. The thirties and forties mark the specifically Romantic period in music. This interval exhibited a pronounced change in form and subject matter, in which all the affinities of Romanticism are to be seen; composers sought effects, designed contrasts and imitations, strove for climaxes, as, like their literary contemporaries, they turned to the expression of bizarre or perverse feeling. All the while, music was taking on a decidedly public character, which manifested itself in the growth of opera and concert. As one student has put it, the nineteenth century brought in the journalist of music, who has served this art in the same way in which he served literature. Music was now fully secular and ready to follow the divergent tendencies of the time.

Especially significant was the steady decay of symphonic form, which effectually mirrored the progressive dissolution of the class system. A modern critic has remarked that "the whole framework of society, whose relation to the individual symbolizes the cadences and codas that gently restrain the flow of Mozart's passionate line, is crumbling away if not already completely desiccated."[1] We are even told that the symphonic form was repellent to Moussorgsky because its first-movement predominance signified to him aristocratic domination.

Music had its Impressionist movement. With Liszt and Debussy, especially, it turned to the exploitation of color and atmosphere and even to the conjuring-up of visual images. This phase was technically a flight from the construction and balance of classical form; in effect it was a concentration upon the "emotive fragments" with which the painters had been occupying themselves.[2]

Thus three broad stages may be recognized in the decline of music in the West. In its highest form this music was architectural; it then became thematic; and, finally, before the incidence of certain present-day reactions, textural. It hardly needs pointing out that this is a movement away from the autonomous and integrated ideal toward a collection of fragments which afford maximum opportunity for subjective and egotistic expression.

I have deferred until last the discussion of jazz, which seems the clearest of all signs of our age's deep-seated predilection for barbarism. The mere fact of its rapid conquest of the world indicates some vast extent of inward ravage, so that there were no real barriers against the disintegration it represents.

Jazz was born in the dives of New Orleans, where the word appears first to have signified an elementary animal function. It was initially a music of primitivism; and we have the word of one of its defenders that "jazz has no need of intelligence; it needs only feeling."[3] But jazz did not remain primitive; something in the Negro's spontaneous manifestation of feeling linked up with Western man's declining faith in the value of culture. The same writer admits that "if one examines the fields of activity which have been reserved for art, one perceives that the creative work of our ancestors was under the impulse of a harmonious equilibrium between reason and sentiment."⁴ Jazz, by formally repudiating restraint by intellect, and by expressing contempt and hostility toward our traditional society and mores, has destroyed this equilibrium. That destruction is a triumph of grotesque, even hysterical, emotion over propriety and reasonableness. Jazz often sounds as if in a rage to divest itself of anything that suggests structure or confinement.

It is understandable, therefore, that jazz should have a great appeal to civilization's fifth column, to the barbarians within the gates. These people found it a useful instrument for the further obliteration of distinctions and the discrediting of all that bears the mark of restraint. Accordingly, it was taken up in a professional way and was sophisticated by artists of technical virtuosity so that it became undeniably a medium of resourcefulness and power. That is all the more reason for recognizing its essential tendency.

The driving impulse behind jazz is best grasped through its syncopation. What this can achieve technically we need not go into here; what it indicates spiritually is a restlessness, a desire to get on, to realize without going through the aesthetic ritual. Forward to the climax, it seems to say; let us dispense with the labor of earning effects. Do we not read in this another form of contempt for labor? Is it not again the modern fatuity of insisting upon the reward without the effort? Form and ritual are outmoded piety, and work is a sacrifice. The primitive and the bored sophisticate are alike impatient for titillation.

As dissent breeds further dissidence, so the emancipation which is jazz gives rise to yet greater vagaries. In "swing" one hears a species of music in which the performer is at fullest liberty to express himself as an egotist. Playing now becomes personal; the musician seizes a theme and improvises as he goes; he develops perhaps a personal idiom, for which he is admired. Instead of that strictness of form which had made the musician like the celebrant of a ceremony, we now have individualization; we hear a variable into which the musician pours his feeling and whimsy more freely than the Romantic poets laid bare their bleeding hearts.

Jazz has been compared to "an indecent story syncopated and counterpointed." There can be no question that, like journalism in literature, it has helped to destroy the concept of obscenity.

In view of such considerations it comes as no surprise to hear a statement that jazz is the music of equality and that it has made important contributions to the fight for freedom. As far as the negative idea of freedom goes, the idea of "freedom from," the case is too clear to need arguing. By dissolving forms, it has left man free to move without reference, expressing dithyrambically whatever surges up from below. It is a music not of dreams—certainly not of our metaphysical dream—but of drunkenness. The higher centers have been proscribed so that the lower may be uninhibited from executing their reeling dance. Here, indeed, is a music to go with empiricism, and it is only natural that the chief devotees of jazz should be the primitive, the young, and those persons, fairly numerous, it would seem, who take pleasure in the thought of bringing down our civilization. The fact that the subjects of jazz, in so far as it may be said to have subjects, are grossly sexual or farcical—subjects of love without aesthetic distance and subjects of comedy without law of proportion—shows how the soul of modern man craves orgiastic disorder. And it is admitted that what man expresses in music dear to him he will most certainly express in his social practices.

Painting too offers its story of what happened to the human psyche in the course of this descent.

If one looks thoughtfully at a gallery of pictures of the modern school, he is likely to notice a peculiar weakness: the theme is not adequate to the craftsmanship. He is observing in another sphere of endeavor the predominance of means over ends. To say that the greatest art must be sustained by story does not mean that it must be "about" something. It would be more accurate to say that topicality occurs after story has been lost. The endless expression of mythology in art which was the achievement of Greece objectifies the metaphysical dream of Greek civilization; its artistic purpose was not to acquaint with story but to utilize story in the creation of significant form. So was it with Christian art. If the proper sentiments are present, there is no need to confuse our appreciation of the topic with our aesthetic appreciation—the mentality which divides over topics and fights battles is symptomatic of disintegration. When a culture is unified on the imaginative level, the unity effects an abridgment of egotism among the members.

The trend toward modernism got under way with the rise of portrait-painting in the fifteenth century. This was followed by the significant development of interest in landscape, which in itself expresses a shift from use of story to interest in technique. The early Renaissance painters had no interest in landscape as such; it was for them mere background, to be formalized and scanted. Because man had not then lost his attribute of divinity, he was for them the center of the world. A thing like "scene," which for the ordinary man of today is likely to stand for the whole of art, they did not even recognize. As painters turned toward landscape and still life, the prevailing interest in the physical world became reflected in art. This trend reached a culmination in the nineteenth century with Impressionism.

The movement of Impressionism, which is the revolutionary event of modern painting, has been attributed to a variety of causes. Clive Bell is inclined to see it simply as a rediscovery of paganism. This meant the acceptance of life as good and satisfying in itself, with a consequent resolution to revel in the here and now. The world of pure sensation thus became the world of art. R. H. Wilenski sees Impressionism as a result of the introduction of the camera and hence, one might say, of the Industrial Revolution. In his view the attempt of the artists to imitate the achievements of a mechanical device degraded perception to mere "seeing." They tried to register vibrations of light as does the camera, and nothing more, though limitations forced upon them one or another kind of architectural synthesis. It has even been suggested that Impressionism served the ends of equalitarian socialism since, if a picture is only the result of exposure to light waves, one tree or field or seascape will be the same for all.

My interpretation is that Impressionism brings nominalism into painting. One of the cardinal tenets of the doctrine is that outline does not exist in nature. Consequently, the main object was "the ultimate divorce of the picture from any convention, whether of arrangement, of drawing, or of a fixed palette."[5] At this point, then, we find the artists, too, applying the doctrine of *universalia post rem*, with which our story first began. If form does not exist prior to things, naturally it is realism to paint things.

In the work that stemmed from this position one sees two important signs of disintegration. The first is this repudiation of form; in their practice the Impressionist painters sought to avoid it by making substance or color perform the whole role. A second and a related sign was the acceptation of ephemerality. It will be found always that those who immerse themselves in substance must also immerse themselves in time. The artists of this school concentrated upon "catching upon canvas the fugitive accents of nature." So Monet, studying changes of light, painted the haystack at nine, at ten-thirty, and again at twelve. Such procedure explains well enough the remark of Baudelaire that art was losing respect for itself as it prostrated before exteriors. The symbolizing of perception through representation was being dropped in favor of an immediate contact with the flux of reality.

It could be asked whether the thesis of this passage is not refuted by the presence of Cézanne in the period under discussion. Now it is true that Cézanne was a great artist and that he consorted with and learned from the Impressionists, but it is not true that finally he was one of them. On the contrary, Cézanne was the first to raise the question of whether sensational truth is the end of art. And the answer to this in the painting of his late period—an answer that dealt with the world through abstraction and simplification—was such that his work has been termed "a pure metaphysical monument." Cézanne is thus an important instance of a phenomenon already observed in literature, wherein the sensitive artist, after brilliant performance within the limits of a vogue, perceives those limits and seeks to transcend them. Such was his course when he professed a hope of making Impressionism as rigorously classical as the Parthenon.

It should cause no astonishment that artists are the first to see that subjectivism and egotism form a cul-de-sac. They are, in the highest sense, the seers; other victims of these maladies stumble along on instinct or seek to rationalize their great errors.

The broad character of the movements we have been following represents a psychic urge to collapse all order, a technical effort to get something without tolerating a medium, which is but another exhibition of the passion for immediacy. Whether we regard the excesses of literary Romanticism, or the syncopation of jazz, or Impressionism in painting, the story is the same. We witness attempts, often ingenious and powerful, to get form without consenting to form, and then we see the beginnings of reaction in symbolism and abstract art.

Egotism in work and art is the flowering, after long growth, of a heresy about human destiny. Its abhorrence of discipline and form is usually grouped with the signs of "progress." It is progress for those who neither have a sense of direction nor want responsibility. The heresy is that man's destiny in the world is not to perfect himself but to lean back in sensual enjoyment. Indeed, there is something expressive of both the philosophy and the technique of artistic Impressionism in the lines from Whitman's *Song of Myself*:

I loaf and invite my soul,
I lean and loaf at my ease observing a spear of summer grass.

The choice was first made in the late Middle Ages, when its fateful nature could be appreciated because cognition still proceeded with reference to ultimates. Progressively it has become a matter of indifference. When masses of men reach a point at which egotism reigns so blandly, can their political damnation be far distant? They have rejected their only guaranty against external control, which is self-discipline, taught and practiced. If they no longer respect community and direct their efforts according to a common understanding, they fall out. Programs like the Four Freedoms, with their vague political unrealism, instead of helping the situation, serve only to codify error. It is the presumption of egotism which renders people unfit for the philosophic anarchy they appear to think of. An ancient axiom of politics teaches that a spoiled people invite despotic control. Their failure to maintain internal discipline is followed by some rationalized organization in the service of a single powerful will. In this particular, at least, history, with all her volumes vast, has but one page.

5

The Great Stereopticon

Sick are they always; they vomit their bile and call it a newspaper.

NIETZSCHE

The disappearance of the primordial synthesis has profound consequences which are felt even by those below the level of philosophy; and it is they, ironically, who make the first effort to repair the damage. It scarcely needs adding that their lack of penetration renders the effort abortive, for what they do, when fragmentation has reached the point of danger, is to attempt a restoration by physical means.

The problem which disintegration places in the lap of practical men, those in charge of states, of institutions, of businesses, is how to persuade to communal activity people who no longer have the same ideas about the most fundamental things. In an age of shared belief, this problem does not exist, for there is a wide area of basic agreement, and dissent is viewed not as a claim to egotistic distinction but as a sort of excommunication. The entire group is conscious of the tendency, which furnishes standards for value judgments. When the goal of life becomes self-realization, however, this vanishes. It vanishes right at that point where the ego asserts its independence; thereafter what reconciliation can there be between authority and individual will? The politicians and businessmen are not interested in saving souls, but they are interested in preserving a minimum of organization, for upon that depend their posts and their incomes. These leaders adopted the liberal's solution to their problem. That was to let religion go but to replace it with education, which supposedly would exercise the same efficacy. The separation of education from religion, one of the proudest achievements of modernism, is but an extension of the separation of knowledge from metaphysics. And the education thus separated can provide their kind of indoctrination. We include here, of course, the education of the classroom, for all such institutionalized instruction proceeds on the assumptions of the state. But the education which best accomplishes their purpose is the systematic indoctrination from day to day of the whole citizenry through channels of information and entertainment.

The vested interests of our age, which, from all kinds of motives, desire to maintain traditional values or to get new values set up in their place, have constructed a wonderful machine, which we shall call the Great Stereopticon. It is the function of this machine to project selected pictures of life in the hope that what is seen will be imitated. All of us of the West who are within the long reach of technology are sitting in the audience. We are told the time to laugh and the time to cry, and signs are not wanting that the audience grows ever more responsive to its cues.

A great point is sometimes made of the fact that modern man no longer sees above his head a revolving dome with fixed stars and glimpses of the *primum mobile*. True enough, but he sees something similar when he looks at his daily newspaper. He sees the events of the day refracted through a medium which colors them as effectively as the cosmology of the medieval scientist determined his view of the starry heavens. The newspaper is a man-made cosmos of the world of events around us at the time. For the average reader it is a construct with a set of significances which he no more thinks of examining than did his pious forebear of the thirteenth century—whom he pities for sitting in medieval darkness—think of questioning the cosmology. This modern man, too, lives under a dome, whose theoretical aspect has been made to harmonize with a materialistic conception of the world. And he employs its conjunctions and oppositions to explain the occurrences of his time with all the confidence of the now supplanted disciple of astrology.

The Great Stereopticon, like most gadgets, has been progressively improved and added to until today it is a machine of three parts: the press, the motion picture, and the radio. Together they present a version of life quite as controlled as that taught by medieval religionists, though feeble in moral inspiration, as we shall see. It is now our object to look at the effects of each in turn.

No one is prepared to understand the influence of journalism on the public mind until he appreciates the fact that the newspaper is a spawn of the machine. A mechanism itself, it has ever been closely linked with the kind of exploitation, financial and political, which accompanies industrialism. The press is the great scribe, possessed of that preponderance of means which technology always provides. The ease with which it multiplies stereotypes makes it the ideal servant of progress. It thrives on an endlessness of dissemination. Its progeny, like the frogs of Egypt, come up into our very kneading troughs. But, just because the mechanical victory of the press is so complete, we are likely to ignore the conditions on which its work proceeds.

I serve notice, therefore, that we here approach a question of blasphemous nature, a question whose mere asking disturbs the deepest complacency of the age. And that is: Has the art of writing proved an unmixed blessing? The thought challenges so many assumptions that to consider it requires almost a fresh orientation in philosophy; but we must recall that it occurred to Plato, who answered the question in the negative. With him it concerned the issue of whether philosophy should be written down, and his conclusion was that philosophy exists best in discourse between persons, the truth leaping up between them "like a flame."

In explanation of this important point he makes Socrates relate a myth about the Egyptian god Theuth, a mighty inventor,
who carried his inventions before King Thamus, desiring that they
be made available to the people. Some of the inventions the King
praised; but he stood firmly against that of writing, declaring that
it could be only a means of propagating false knowledge and an
encouragement to forgetfulness. Socrates adds the view that anyone who leaves writing behind on the supposition that it will be
"intelligible or certain" or who believes that writing is better than
knowledge present to the mind is badly mistaken.

Now Plato was disturbed by written discourse because it has
"no reticences or proprieties toward different classes of persons"
and because, if an individual goes to it with a question in his mind,
it "always gives one unvarying answer." And we find him making
in the seventh *Epistle* the extraordinary statement that "no intelligent man will ever be so bold as to put into language those things
which his reason has contemplated, especially not into a form that
is unalterable,—which must be the case with what is expressed in
written symbols." Obviously, here is a paradox, and the present
writer is aware of risking another in a book which calls attention to the sin of writing. The answer to the problem seems to be
that written discourse *is* under a limitation and that whether we
wish to accept that limitation to secure other advantages must be
decided after due reference to purposes and circumstances. In the
Good Society it is quite possible that man will not be so dependent
on the written word.

In any case, for Plato, truth was a living thing, never wholly
captured by men even in animated discourse and in its purest form,
certainly, never brought to paper. In our day it would seem that a
contrary presumption has grown up. The more firmly an utterance
is stereotyped, the more likely it is to win credit. It is assumed that
engines as expensive and as powerful as the modern printing press
will naturally be placed in the hands of men of knowledge. Faith in
the printed word has raised journalists to the rank of oracles; yet

could there be a better description of them than these lines from
the *Phaedrus*: "They will appear to be omniscient and will generally know nothing; they will be tiresome, having the reputation of
knowledge without the reality"?

If the realization of truth is the product of a meeting of minds,
we may be skeptical of the physical ability of the mechanism to
propagate it as long as that propagation is limited to the printing
and distribution of stories which give "one unvarying answer."
And this circumstance brings up at once the question of the intention of the rulers of the press. There is much to indicate that
modern publication wishes to minimize discussion. Despite many
artful pretensions to the contrary, it does not want an exchange of
views, save perhaps on academic matters. Instead, it encourages
men to read in the hope that they will absorb. For one thing, there
is the technique of display, with its implied evaluations. This does
more of the average man's thinking for him than he suspects. For
another, there is the stereotyping of whole phrases. These are carefully chosen not to stimulate reflection but to evoke stock responses
of approbation or disapprobation. Headlines and advertising teem
with them, and we seem to approach a point at which failure to
make the stock response is regarded as faintly treasonable, like
refusal to salute the flag. Especially do the journals of mass cir-
culation exploit the automatic response. So journalism becomes a
monstrous discourse of Protagoras, which charms by hypnotizing
and thwarts that participation without which one is not a thinking
man. If our newspaper reader were trained to look for assumptions, if he were conscious of the rhetoric in lively reporting, we
might not fear this product of the printer's art; but that would be
to grant that he is educated. As the modern world is organized, the
ordinary reader seems to lose means of private judgment, and the
decay of conversation has about destroyed the practice of dialectic.
Consequently the habit of credulity grows.

There is yet another circumstance which raises grave doubts
about the contribution of journalism to the public weal. News-

papers are under strong pressure to distort in the interest of holding attention. I think we might well afford to overlook the pressure of advertisers upon news and editorial policy. This source of distortion has been fully described and is perhaps sufficiently discounted; but there is at work a far more insidious urge to exaggerate and to color beyond necessity. It is an inescapable fact that newspapers thrive on friction and conflict. One has only to survey the headlines of some popular journal, often presented symbolically in red, to note the *kind* of thing which is considered news. Behind the big story there nearly always lies a battle of some sort. Conflict, after all, is the essence of drama, and it is a truism that newspapers deliberately start and prolong quarrels; by allegation, by artful quotation, by the accentuation of unimportant differences, they create antagonism where none was felt to exist before. And this is profitable practically, for the opportunity to dramatize a fight is an opportunity for news. Journalism, on the whole, is glad to see a quarrel start and sorry to see it end. In the more sensational publications this spirit of passion and violence, manifested in a certain recklessness of diction, with vivid verbs and fortissimo adjectives, creeps into the very language. By the attention it gives their misdeeds it makes criminals heroic and politicians larger than life. I have felt that the way in which newspapers raked over every aspect of Adolf Hitler's life and personality since the end of the war shows that they really have missed him; they now have no one to play anti-Christ against the bourgeois righteousness they represent.

In reviewing the persistent tendency of the newspaper to corrupt, I shall cite a passage from James Fenimore Cooper. Though Cooper lived before the advent of yellow journalism, he seems to have stated the essential situation with a truth and eloquence impossible to improve on when he said in *The American Democrat*: "As the press of this country now exists, it would seem to be expressly devised by the great agent of mischief, to depress and destroy all that is good, and to elevate and advance all that is evil in the nation. The little truth that is urged, is usually urged coarsely,

weakened and rendered vicious, by personalities; while those who
live by falsehoods, fallacies, enmities, partialities and the schemes
of the designing, find the press the very instrument that the devils
would invent to effect their designs." A hundred years later Huey
Long made a statement of impolitic truth when he called his tax
on newspapers a "lie tax."

How, in the light of these facts, can one hesitate to conclude that
we would live in greater peace and enjoy sounder moral health if
the institution of the newspaper were abolished entirely? Jefferson
observed at one time that it would be better to have newspapers
and lack a government than to have a government and be without
newspapers. Yet we find him in his seventieth year writing to John
Adams: "I have given up newspapers in exchange for Tacitus and
Thucydides, for Newton and Euclid, and I find myself much the
happier."

The Russians, with their customary logical realism, which ought
to come as a solemn admonition to the Western mind, have concluded that freedom to initiate conflicts is not one of the legitimate
freedoms. They have therefore established state control of journalism. If newspapers can do nothing but lie, they will at least lie in
the interest of the state, which, according to the philosophy of statism, is not lying at all. Certainly it remains to be seen whether the
Western democracies with their strong divisive forces can continue
to allow a real freedom of the press. In limited areas, indeed, there
are now signs that the day of that freedom is over.

We see this silently arising in the appearance of the press agent
and the public-relations officer. More institutions of every kind are
coming to feel that they cannot permit an unrestricted access to
news about themselves. What they do is simply set up an office of
publicity in which writers skilled in propaganda prepare the kinds
of stories those institutions wish to see circulated. Inevitably this
organization serves at the same time as an office of censorship, de-
emphasizing, or withholding entirely, news which would be damaging to prestige. It is easy, of course, to disguise such an office

as a facility created to keep the public better informed, but this does not alter the fact that where interpretation counts, control of source is decisive. During the second World War the United States government set up a vast office of war information, the object of which was to interpret the struggle from the point of view of an administration which had been all along pro-war. In this day of skilled competition for public favor, even separate departments of government have their public information services. I shall illustrate by citing in some detail from a recent press dispatch from Washington: "The United States Navy, which in pre-war days hid its light under a bushel, has decided to embark on a high-powered publicity program." Its plan, the account goes on to say, is to gather a staff of five hundred men the duties of which will be to provide "photographs, radio programs, and other public information about the navy." The development resulted, it is explained, from a realization that during the war "the publicity machines of the army and the army air forces were able to capture public support to the detriment of the navy's reputation." In the course of the war, this candid correspondent declares, the Navy made some effort to get in step with the times when it "introduced modern advertising agency methods and discarded the traditional name of 'office of public relations' for the more euphemistic 'office of public information.'" Such is the policy of seeing that there is enough news and that it originates in the proper hands. The practice is becoming universal; not only departments of governments and private businesses but even universities have concluded that freedom of access to news turns out to be expensive and embarrassing.

So much for forces which keep this part of the Stereopticon from giving us the living truth; now let us turn to the second part.

Every student of the motion picture has been impressed with the great resourcefulness of this medium. The movie producer is a maker almost to the extent of the poet, for he is working with a means capable of transforming subject matter. His production carries the evaluative power implicit in all dramatic representation, and it is, in the usual course of affairs, employed for purposes of entertainment. These two points bear consideration.

We need not speak of the enormous influence of this synoptic depiction of life upon children and adolescents. That is a point concerning reticences and proprieties toward different classes of persons; our interest is rather in the deleterious effects of movie-going upon even adult mentalities that find satisfaction in it. That the public as a whole misses the issue of the motion picture's influence can be seen from its attitude toward censorship. For what the public is reconciled to seeing censored are just the little breaches of decorum which fret bourgeois respectability and sense of security. The truth is that these are so far removed from the heart of the problem that they could well be ignored. The thing that needs to be censored is not the length of the kisses but the egotistic, selfish, and self-flaunting hero; not the relative proportion of undraped breast but the flippant, vacuous-minded, and also egotistic hero-ine. Let us not worry about the jokes of dubious propriety; let us rather object to the whole story, with its complacent assertion of the virtues of materialist society. We are speaking here, of course, from the fundamental point of view. A censorship of the movies, to be worthy of the name, would mean a complete reinterpretation of most of their themes, for the beliefs which underlie virtually every movie story are precisely the ones which are hurrying us on to perdition. The entire globe is becoming imbued with the notion that there is something normative about the insane sort of life lived in New York and Hollywood—even after that life has been exaggerated to suit the morbid appetite of the thrill-seeker.

The spurious nature of the "interest" of the ordinary movie shows an indifference to the real issues of life. The producer, in order to make his offerings attractions, that is, in order to make them beguiling, must present them as slick and false as advertising. It has been said that tragedy is for aristocrats, comedy is for bourgeoisie, and farce is for peasants. What percentage of the output of motion-picture factories can qualify as tragedy?[1] With the animated cartoon, a growing percentage qualifies as farce. But romance and comedy—these measure the depth of the world which movie audiences wish to see.

The third part of the Great Stereopticon is the radio and television. Because they bring the human voice, unique opportunities are open to them.

The primary effect of the radio is to disorder further our picture of the world by diminishing the opportunity for genuine selection (in its system of programs it has achieved a "rationalization" which results in the wildly irrational). One skims through a newspaper, practicing a certain art of rejection; the movie he may stay away from, but the radio is insistently present; indeed the victims of this publicity are virtually hunted down. In few public places do we escape it, and our neighbor's loud-speaker may penetrate the very sanctum of our privacy. In our listening, voluntary or not, we are made to grow accustomed to the weirdest of juxtapositions: the serious and the trivial, the comic and the tragic, follow one another in mechanical sequence without real transition. During the recent war what person of feeling was not struck by the insanity of hearing advertisements for laxatives between announcements of the destruction of famous cities by aerial bombardment? Is it not a travesty of all sense to hear reports fraught with disaster followed by the comedy-variety with its cheap wit and arranged applause (this applause, of course, tells the listeners when to react and how and so further submerges them in massness).[2]

Here, it would seem, is the apotheosis; here is the final collapsing of values, a fantasia of effects, suggesting in its wild disorder the debris left by a storm. Here is the daily mechanical wrecking of hierarchy.

Not to be overlooked in any gauging of influence is the voice of announcer and commentator. The metaphysical dream of progress dictates the tone, which is one of cheery confidence, assuring us in the face of all contrary evidence that the best is yet to be. Recalling the war years once more, who has not heard the news of some terrible tragedy, which might stagger the imagination and cause the conscientious artist to hesitate at the thought of its depiction, given to the world in the same tone that commends a brand of soap or predicts fair weather for the morrow? There were commentators, it is true, who got the spirit of gravity into their speech, but behind them stood always the announcer, denying by his formula of regular inflection the poignancy of their message. The radio, more than press or screen, is the cheerful liar.

Thus the broadcast of chaos comes in a curious monotone. This is the voice of the Hollow Men, who can see the toppling walls of Jerusalem, Athens, and Rome without enough soul to sense tragedy. It is the tone of those dead to sentiment. But this is as we predicted; the closer man stands to ruin, the duller grows his realization; the annihilation of spiritual being precedes the destruction of temple walls.

The radio is, last of all, a prime instrument for discouraging the thought of participation. It is the natural monopoly of communication. For turning whole populations into mute recipients of authoritative edicts, what better means could there be? A national radio hookup is like the loud-speaker system of a battleship or a factory, from which the post of command can transmit orders to every part. If we grant the assumptions of the materialists that society must conform to the developments of science, we may as well prepare ourselves for the monolithic state.

Thus far we have been speaking of specific temptations to suppress and distort; it is now time to look at the fundamental source of the harm done by the Great Stereopticon. If we are pleading for unity of mind and if we admit the necessity for some degree of subjective determination, it might appear that this machine, with its power to make the entire environment rhetorical, is a heaven-sent answer to our needs. We do not in the final reckoning desire un-interpreted data; it is precisely the interpretation which holds our interest. But the great fault is that data, as it passes through the machine, takes its significance from a sickly metaphysical dream.

The ultimate source of evaluation ceases to be the dream of beauty and truth and becomes that of psychopathia, of fragmentation, of disharmony and nonbeing. The operators of the Stereopticon by their very selection of matter make horrifying assumptions about reality. For its audience that overarching dome becomes a sort of miasmic cloud, a breeder of strife and degradation and of the subhuman. What person taking the affirmative view of life can deny that the world served up daily by press, movie, and radio is a world of evil and negation? There is iron in our nature sufficient to withstand any fact that is present in a context of affirmation, but we cannot remain unaffected by the continued assertion of cynicism and brutality. Yet these are what the materialists in control of publicity give us.

The sickly metaphysical dream is not the creation solely of those who have cast restraint to the winds to seek profit in sensationalism. It is the work, too, of many who profess higher ideals but who cannot see where their assumptions lead. Fundamental to the dream, of course, is the dogma of progress, with its postulate of the endlessness of becoming. The habit of judging all things by their departure from the things of yesterday is reflected in most journalistic interpretation. Hence the restlessness and the criteria of magnitude and popularity. The fact that capitalism seems to flourish only by expansion is no doubt connected with this; but, whatever the cause may be, there is no law of perfection where there are no standards of measure. The touchstone of progress simply schools the millions in shallow evaluation.

Somewhere, moreover, the metaphysicians of publicity have absorbed the idea that the goal of life is happiness through comfort. It is a state of complacency supposed to ensue when the physical appetites have been well satisfied. Advertising fosters the concept, social democracy approves it, and the acceptance is so wide that it is virtually impossible today, except from the religious rostrum, to teach that life means discipline and sacrifice. It means, in the world picture of press agency, a job, domesticity, interest in some harmless diversion such as baseball and fishing, and a strong antipathy toward abstract ideas. This is the Philistine version of man in pursuit of happiness. Even Carlyle's doctrine of blessedness through work has overtones of strenuousness which are repugnant to the man of today. Because the journalist-philosophers evaluate the multifarious objects and events of the world by their appeal to the greatest possible number of this type, it is not to be expected that they will recommend the arduous road of spiritualization.

As for the latter, it cannot be said too emphatically that the operators of the Great Stereopticon have an interest in keeping people from breaking through to deeper significances. Not only is the philosopher a notoriously poor consumer; he is also an unsettling influence on societies careless of justice. That there are abysses of meaning beneath his daily routine, the common man occasionally suspects; to have him realize them in some apocalyptic revelation might well threaten the foundations of materialist civilization. It is no wonder that experienced employers advertise for workers who are married and sober, for the other type sometimes begins to wonder which is the *real* reality, and they cannot afford help which might behave as Santayana, when he reportedly deserted the Harvard lecture room at the voice of spring, or Sherwood Anderson, when he left without adieu the Ohio paint factory.

The speculations of journalism seldom go beyond the confines of business and propriety, and its oracles have been quick to assail those who come with disturbing notions—quick and unscrupulous, too, if they sense that the notions contain some necessary truth. In this they bear out the observation of Socrates that society does not mind an individual's being wise; only when he begins to make others wise does it become apprehensive. This is to say that they fear the spread of what has truth and reason on its side. Has any brilliant social critic of the last century received something better than a sneer from the pundits of journalism until his appreciation by the thoughtful forced a grudging recognition? A Nietzsche, a Kierkegaard, a Péguy, a Spengler—it is impossible for journalism to take these people seriously. The existence of the one threatens the existence of the other. The proprietors of the Stereopticon have a pretty clear idea of the level at which thinking is safe for the established order. They are protecting a materialist civilization growing more insecure and panicky as awareness filters through that it is over an abyss.

Thus, by insisting upon the dogma of progress, by picturing physical sufficiency as the goal of living, by insulating the mind against thoughts of an immanent reality, the Great Stereopticon keeps the ordinary citizen from perceiving "the vanity of his book-keeping and the emptiness of his domestic felicities." It is the great projection machine of the bourgeois mentality, which we have already seen to be psychopathic in its alienation from reality.

It is curious to see how this mentality impresses those brought up under differing conditions. I recall with especial vividness a passage from Walter Hines Page's *The Autobiography of Nicholas Worth*. Page, who grew up in the Reconstruction South and later went North to school, had received his earliest impressions in a society where catastrophe and privation had laid bare some of the primal realities, including the existence of evil—a society, too, in which the "primitive infection" of the African race, to use a term employed by Jung, had developed in the white man some psychological cunning. It seemed to Page that his northern acquaintances had "minds of logical simplicity."[3] Such, I think, must be the feeling of anyone who comes out of a natural environment into one in which education, however lengthy and laborious, is based on bourgeois assumptions about the real character of the world. It is a mind which learns to play with counters and arrives at answers which work—in a bourgeois environment. If we reverse this process and send the "mind of logical simplicity" into regions where mystery and contingency are recognized, we re-enact the plot of Conrad's *Lord Jim*. There is a world of terrifying reality to which the tidy moralities of an Anglican parsonage do not seem applicable.[4]

Seen from another point of view, the Great Stereopticon is a translation into actuality of Plato's celebrated figure of the cave. The defect of the prisoners, let us recall, is that they cannot perceive the truth. The wall before them, on which the shadows play, is the screen on which press, motion picture, and radio project their account of life. The chains which keep the prisoners from turning their heads are the physical monopoly which the engines of publicity naturally possess. And is it not pathetically true that these victims, with their limited vision, are "in the habit of conferring honors among themselves to those who are quickest to observe the passing shadows and to remark which of them went before and which followed after, and which were together"?

The result is that insulation by technology has made the task of disseminating wisdom more difficult since Plato's day. In Athenian sophistry and demagoguery Plato faced evils of the same kind, but they could not work behind such strategic entrenchment, and it was hardly as difficult for the wise man to make himself heard in centers of influence. Nothing is more natural than that, in an age dominated by materialism, authority should attach to those who possess. What chance today, to make the situation concrete, has a street-corner preacher, without means and without institutional sponsorship, in competition with the glib assertions of a radio oracle? The denizens of the cave have never been so firmly enchained as in this age, which uses liberty as a veritable incantation.

There are, it is true, certain hopeful signs of restiveness growing out of our condition. Most of us have observed among ordinary people a deep suspicion of propaganda since the first World War. The lesson of that disillusionment has lasted surprisingly. So intense has been this distrust that during the recent conflict the most authentic stories of outrages, documented and proved in every possible way, either were met with outright disbelief or were accepted gingerly and with reservations. The common man realizes that he has been misled and that there are those who would mislead him again; but, lacking analytical power, he tends to group every instance of organized expression with propaganda. In times of peace, too, he has exhibited a certain hardheaded resistance to attempts to drive or cajole him. We have seen in this country politicians elected in the face of almost unanimous press opposition; we note oftentimes a cagey dismissal of the obvious falsification in advertising, and I have heard simple men remark that newspapers should not print items of a private and distressing nature such as we have classified as obscene.

In serious writing, too, there are some hopeful portents of change. It has been noted how modern poets have reacted against the debased coinage of cliché language; and indications appear in other types of literature that the middle-class world picture is being abandoned. Perhaps Arthur Koestler is right: as the bourgeois novel flickers out, an entirely new type of writer is destined to appear: "airmen, revolutionaries, adventurers, men who lead the dangerous life." Such, indeed, seem Silone, Saint-Exupéry, Hemingway. They will carry the gift for reflection into experiences of intense physical distress, and they will emerge with a more genuine contempt for materialist explanations than has been seen for centuries. When Saint-Exupéry, for example, declares that "the physical drama itself cannot touch us until someone points out its spiritual sense," he makes an affirmation of tragedy and significance. In a way, these men have the same recourse as medieval mystics, who, in suffering, caught the vision. And, since their faith has been tested by fire, they cannot be intimidated by those things which reduce the armchair philosopher to meekness. They have broken through the falsity and have returned to tell that the world is not at all what it has been made to seem—not after one has cut loose from security and comfort and achieved a kind of freedom far different from that promised by political liberals, who are themselves pushing slides into the Stereopticon. In reflecting on what is taught by extremities, one is reminded of Yeats's saying that saints and drunkards are never Whigs.

It will certainly have to be asked whether European fascism

was not just this impulse vulgarized and perverted. The rebellion of youth, the repudiation of bourgeois complacency, the attempt to renew the sense of "holiness and heroism," appear the beginning of a revolt at least as deep-seated as that which made the French Revolution. The revolt was led by ignorant spirits who were impelled from behind by resentment and who, through their determination to invert the Christian ethic, made an unexampled fiasco. There is no reason to believe, however, that the deep dissatisfaction with the superficiality of Western life has been removed or even mitigated. And this is why we wonder how long the Stereopticon can preserve the inane world which the bourgeois finds congenial. It is, after all, only a mechanical means of unifying empirical communities.

In summary, the plea that the press, motion picture, and radio justify themselves by keeping people well informed turns out to be misleading. If one thinks merely of facts and of vivid sensations, the claim has some foundation, but if he thinks of encouragement to meditation, the contrary rather is true. For by keeping the time element continuously present—and one may recall Henry James's description of journalism as criticism of the moment at the moment—they discourage composition and so promote the fragmentation already reviewed. We have seen in other connections how specialization is hostile to all kinds of organization, whether that organization is expressed as image, as whole, or as generalization. In the last analysis this reveals itself as an attempt to prevent the simultaneous perception of successive events, which is the achievement of the philosopher. Materialism and success require the "decomposed eternity" of time for their operation, and this is why we have these hidden but persistent attacks on memory, which holds successive events in a single picture. The successive perception of successive events is empiricism; the simultaneous perception is idealism. Need we go further to account for the current dislike of long memories and for the hatred of the past?

Recurring to Plato's observation that a philosopher must have a good memory, let us inquire whether the continuous dissemination, of news by the media under discussion does not produce the provincial in time. The constant stream of sensation, eulogized as lively propagation of what the public wants to hear, discourages the pulling-together of events from past time into a whole for contemplation. Thus, absence of reflection keeps the individual from being aware of his former selves, and it is highly questionable whether anyone can be a member of a metaphysical community who does not preserve such memory. Upon the presence of the past in the present depends all conduct directed by knowledge.

There can be little doubt that this condition of mind is a large factor in the low political morality of our age.

Oswald Garrison Villard, a political journalist of the old school, who spent half a century crusading for standards of probity in public administration, once declared that he had never ceased to marvel at the shortness of the public's memory, at the rapidity with which it forgets episodes of scandal and incompetence. It sometimes appeared to him of little use to attack a party for its unethical conduct, for the voters would have no recollection of it. The glee with which the epithet "ancient history" is applied to what is out of sight is of course a part of this barbarous attitude. The man of culture finds the whole past relevant; the bourgeois and the barbarian find relevant only what has some pressing connection with their appetites. Those who remember alone have a sense of relatedness, but whoever has a sense of relatedness is in at least the first grade of philosophy. Henry Ford's statement that history is bunk is a perfectly proper observation for a bourgeois industrialist, and it was followed with equal propriety by another: "Creeds must go." Technology emancipates not only from memory but also from faith.

What humane spirit, after reading a newspaper or attending a popular motion picture or listening to the farrago of nonsense on a radio program, has not found relief in fixing his gaze upon some characteristic bit of nature? It is escape from the sickly metaphysical dream. Out of the surfeit of falsity born of technology and commercialism we rejoice in returning to primary data and to assurance that the world is a world of enduring forms which in themselves are neither brutal nor sentimental.

6

The Spoiled-Child Psychology

Wherever the typical mass character becomes universal, all higher
values are as good as lost.

RAUSCHNING

Having been taught for four centuries, more or less, that his redemption lies through the conquest of nature, man expects his
heaven to be spatial and temporal, and, beholding all things
through the Great Stereopticon, he expects redemption to be easy
of attainment. Only by these facts can we explain the spoiled-child
psychology of the urban masses. The scientists have given him the
impression that there is nothing he cannot know, and false propa-
gandists have told him that there is nothing he cannot have. Since
the prime object of the latter is to appease, he has received conces-
sions at enough points to think that he may obtain what he wishes
through complaints and demands. This is but another phase of the
rule of desire.

The spoiled child has not been made to see the relationship between effort and reward. He wants things, but he regards payment
as an imposition or as an expression of malice by those who with-
hold for it. His solution, as we shall see, is to abuse those who do
not gratify him.

No one can be excused for moral degradation, but we are

tempted to say of the urban dweller, as of the heathen, that he never had an opportunity for salvation. He has been exposed so unremittingly to this false interpretation of life that, though we may deplore, we can hardly wonder at the unreasonableness of his demands. He has been given the notion that progress is automatic, and hence he is not prepared to understand impediments; and the right to pursue happiness he has not unnaturally translated into a right to have happiness, like a right to the franchise. If all this had been couched in terms of spiritual insight, the case would be different, but when he is taught that happiness is obtainable in a world limited to surfaces, he is being prepared for that disillusionment and resentment which lay behind the mass psychosis of fascism. He has been told in substance that the world is conditioned, and when unconditioned forces enter to put an end to his idyl, he naturally suffers frustration. His superiors in the hierarchy of technology have practiced an imposition upon him, and in periodic crises he calls them to account.

Let us consider an ordinary man living in Megalopolis. The Stereopticon has so shielded him from sight of the abysses that he conceives the world to be a fairly simple machine, which, with a bit of intelligent tinkering, can be made to go. And going, it turns out comforts and whatever other satisfactions his demagogic leaders have told him he is entitled to. But the mysteries are always intruding, so that even the best designed machine has been unable to effect a continuous operation. No less than his ancestors, he finds himself up against toil and trouble. Since this was not nominated in the bond, he suspects evildoers and takes the childish course of blaming individuals for things inseparable from the human condition. The truth is that he has never been brought to see what it is to be a man. That man is the product of discipline and of forging, that he really owes thanks for the pulling and tugging that enable him to grow—this concept left the manuals of education with the advent of Romanticism. This citizen is now the child of indulgent parents who pamper his appetites and inflate his egotism until he is unfitted for struggle of any kind.

The spoiling of man seems always to begin when urban living predominates over rural. After man has left the countryside to shut himself up in vast piles of stone, after he has lost what Sir Thomas Browne called *pudor rusticus*, after he has come to depend on a complicated system of human exchange for his survival, he becomes forgetful of the overriding mystery of creation. Such is the normal condition of the *déraciné*. An artificial environment causes him to lose sight of the great system not subject to man's control. Undoubtedly this circumstance is a chief component of bourgeois mentality, as even the etymology of "bourgeois" may remind us. It is the city-dweller, solaced by man-made comforts, who resents the very thought that there exist mighty forces beyond his understanding; it is he who wishes insulation and who berates and persecutes the philosophers, the prophets and mystics, the wild men out of the desert, who keep before him the theme of human frailty.

It is part of his desiccation to substitute for the primal feeling of relatedness a false self-sufficiency. If he could continue to realize the presence of something greater than self and see the virtue of subordinating self to communal enterprise—that is, see the virtue and not simply respond to coercion—he might remain unspoiled even in the city. But, when competition to be considered "equal" sets in, there ensues the severance which is individualism. It has proved as true of the spirit as of the flesh that the city renders sterile.

This fact has been discerned in many societies, but in our own it takes on an added liability through the expansion of science. If cities encourage man to believe that he is superior to the limitations of nature, science encourages him to believe that he is exempt from labor. In effect, what modern man is being told is that the world owes him a living. He assents the more readily for being told in a roundabout way, which is that science owes him a living. The city will shelter him, and science will support him; what more is required by the dream of utilitarianism? And what possible lesson can man draw from this but that work is a curse, which he will avoid as far as possible until science arrives with the means for its total abolishment? When men must no longer win bread by the sweat of their brow, the primal curse will have ceased; and we are assured daily by advertisements that the goal is not too far off.

How obvious here is the extinction of the idea of mission. Men no longer feel it laid upon them to translate the potential into the actual; there are no goals of labor like those of the cathedral-builders. Yet, unless man sees himself in relation to ordinances such as these, what lies ahead is the most egregious self-pampering and self-disgust, probably followed by real illness. With religion emasculated, it has remained for medical science in our age to revive the ancient truth that labor is therapeutic.

The polarity of the actual and the potential creates a tension in the presence of which complete comfort is impossible. Here is the secret of the mass man's impatience with ideals. Certainly there is no more innocent-seeming form of debauchery than the worship of comfort; and, when it is accompanied by a high degree of technical resourcefulness, the difficulty of getting people not to renounce it but merely to see its consequences is staggering. The task is bound up, of course, with that of getting principles accepted again, for, where everything ministers to desire, there can be no rebuke to comfort.

As we endeavor to restore values, we need earnestly to point out that there is no correlation between the degree of comfort enjoyed and the achievement of a civilization. On the contrary, absorption in ease is one of the most reliable signs of present or impending decay. Greek civilization, to take an outstanding example, was notably deficient in creature comforts. The Athenians sat outdoors on stone to behold their tragedies; the modern New Yorker sits in an inclined plush armchair to witness some play properly classified as amusement. When the Greek retired for the night, it was not to a beautyrest mattress; he wrapped himself up in his cloak and lay down on a bench like a third-class railway passenger, as Clive Bell has remarked. Nor had he learned to pity himself for a spare diet. Privations of the flesh were no obstacle to his marvelous world of imagination.

On the other hand, how many Americans have returned from Europe with terrible tales of the chill and draftiness of medieval castles and Renaissance palaces, with stories of deficient plumbing and uncomfortable chairs! Mark Twain was right to make his Connecticut Yankee score the lack of conveniences in Camelot. Yet it is just such people who will remain indifferent to the drabness of Gopher Prairie and Zenith and find their mental pabulum in drugstore fiction.

Culture consists, in truth, of many little things; but they are not armrests and soft beds and extravagant bathing facilities. These, after all, cater to sensation, and, because culture is of the imagination, the man of culture is to a degree living out of this world.

The worship of comfort, then, is only another aspect of our decision to live wholly in this world. Yet here man encounters an anomaly: the very policy of living wholly in this world, of having no traffic with that other world which cannot be "proved," turns one's attention wholly to the temporary and so actually impairs his effectiveness. We may feel satisfied to be damned for not producing great art or for not observing ceremony, but what if it is shown that addiction to comfort unfits us for survival? This is not a new story; the fate of the fat and flabby animal overtaken by the lean and hungry presents an allegory of familiar experience. Nor is it necessary to review the days of Roman degeneracy, though the case would be apposite; let us rather see the problem in its essence and ask whether the worship of comfort does not follow necessarily from loss of belief in ideas and thereby induce social demoralization. The fact that it originates with the middle class, with those who would be moderate even in virtue, as Nietzsche remarked, is significant. After a people have repudiated ideals, they respond to the prick of appetite as an animal to a goad, but this, for reasons already outlined, does not take the place of systematic labor toward a suprapersonal goal. In becoming pragmatic, they become ineffectual. De Tocqueville, alert to discern the effects of different social ideals, noted this well: "In ages of faith, the final end of life is placed beyond life. The men of those ages, therefore, naturally and almost involuntarily accustom themselves to fix their gaze for many years on some immovable object toward which they are constantly tending; and they learn by insensible degrees to repress a multitude of petty passing desires in order to be the better able to content that great and lasting desire which possesses them. . . . This explains why religious nations have often achieved such lasting results; for whilst they were thinking only of the other world, they had found out the great secret of success in this."

Great architectonic ideas are not nourished by the love of comfort, yet science is constantly telling the masses that the future will be better because the conditions of life are going to be softened. With this softening, the masculine virtue of heroism becomes, like the sentiments of which Burke spoke, "absurd and antiquated."

The way was prepared for the criteria of comfort and mediocrity when the Middle Ages abandoned the ethic of Plato for that of Aristotle. The latter's doctrine of rational prudence compelled him to declare in the *Politics* that the state is best ruled by the middle class. For him, the virtuous life was an avoidance of extremes, a middle course between contraries considered harmful. Such doctrine leaves out of account the possibility that there are some virtues which do not become defective through increase, that virtues like courage and generosity may be pursued to an end at which man effaces himself. Naturally the idea of self-effacement will be absent from any philosophy which prescribes for a prosperous worldly career.

Here the conception of Plato—expressed certainly, too, by Christianity—of pursuing virtue until worldly consequence becomes a matter of indifference, stands in contrast. Aristotle remains a kind of natural historian of the virtues, observing and recording them as he observed techniques of the drama, but not thinking of a spiritual ideal. A life accommodated to this world and shunning the painful experiences which extremes, including those of virtue, entail was what he proposed for his son Nicomachus.

One could anticipate that this theory would recommend itself to the Renaissance gentlemen and later to the bourgeoisie when their turn came. In Thomism, based as it is on Aristotle, even the Catholic church turned away from the asceticism and the rigorous morality of the patristic fathers to accept a degree of pragmatic acquiescence in the world. This difference has prompted someone to say that, whereas Plato built the cathedrals of England, Aristotle built the manor houses.

The trend continues, and in a modern document like the Four Freedoms one sees comfort and security embodied in canons. For the philosophic opposition, that is of course proper, because fascism taught the strenuous life. But others with spiritual aims in mind have taught it too. Emerson made the point: "Heroism, like Plotinus, is almost ashamed of its body. What shall it say, then, to the sugar plums and cat's cradles, to the toilet, compliments, quarrels, cards, and custard, which rack the wit of all human society?" Since he who longs to achieve does not ask whether the seat is soft or the weather at a pleasant temperature, it is obvious that hardness is a condition of heroism. Exertion, self-denial, endurance, these make the hero, but to the spoiled child they connote the evil of nature and the malice of man.

The modern temper is losing the feeling for heroism even in war, which used to afford the supreme theme for celebration of this virtue. It is significant that, whereas wars were formerly spoken of as crusades or, at least, as trials, it was the practice in America to refer to World War II as a "job." These little changes in speech are as revealing as changes in dress. It was a "job" to be done so that the boys could get home to their bourgeois existences, which had not contemplated such a cataclysm, and which had no nomenclature for it when it arrived. The organs of propaganda were hard put to convince the public that this was not just an ordinary job, since the reward was at best in intangibles and since there might be no reward at all. Thus we saw the constant reference to soldiers' and workers' hours and pay, in an effort to make the soldier see that he was fighting for something more than fifty dollars a month and to persuade the factory worker that the measure of his performance was not the wage earned but what was being turned out for the front. It was an organized campaign, using all the resources of the Great Stereopticon to bring home to a people gone materialist the truth that sacrifice means not investment but giving up something to the transcendental.

During the early part of the second World War there came to light the story of a farmer from the back country of Oklahoma— one of the yet unspoiled—who, upon hearing of the attack on Pearl Harbor, departed with his wife to the West Coast to work in the shipyards. His wife found employment as a waitress and supported the two. Unable to read, the new worker did not understand the meaning of the little slip of paper handed him once a week. It was not until he had accumulated over a thousand dollars in checks that he found out that he was being paid to save his country. He had assumed that when the country is in danger, everyone helps out, and helping out means giving.

On the other side, there is meaning in the one popular ballad to come out of World War II. "Roger Young" has the line, "O we've got no time for glory in the infantry." The language of business was increasingly applied to war, as when "soldier" and "sailor" were displaced by the neuter "servicemen." To say "Our boy is in service" instead of "Our son is fighting for his native land" pretty well empties out the heroic strain.

The war of unlimited objectives which the democracies waged at the end may, in fact, be explained by the rage they felt over having their comfort disrupted and the contingent nature of their world exposed. In this rage they made the egregious mistake of supposing that "unconditional" war is a means of doing away with all war. That may turn out to have been part of their unfitness.

So much for physical conflict; now we must pause to ask whether the spoiled-child psychology does not unfit us also for that political struggle which now seems to loom inexorable. We have reference, naturally, to the new balance of power between East and West, between bourgeois liberal democracy and Soviet communism. With their ideal of happiness through comfort, the Western people look forward to an era of undisturbed living, in which such progress as their metaphysic demands will take the form of a conquest of nature. These conquests are threat enough to the prized equilibrium, if the truth were understood, but they may be little in comparison with the ideology fostered by their great rival to the East. For, however much the Bolsheviks have bemused themselves with other sophistries, they have never lost sight of the fact that life is a struggle. And, since they see expansion as the price of survival, they are wholly committed to dynamism. To the leaders of Eastern communism there is no such thing as a "good-neighbor policy" in our sense. That would involve a respect for abstract rights. How they must chuckle over this fatuity of liberalism. They see the world in a mighty evolution, in which the abstract rights of individuals and of nations go down before irresistible processes.

It is mainly this which makes the "blue heaven" of the Western liberals so precarious. What are the inalienable rights, by which they demonstrate their claim to happiness, to that power whose metaphysical dream is dynamism? Even if we could assume pacific intentions on both sides, the future would not be safe for Western liberalism. Its fundamental incapacity to think, arising from an inability to see contradictions, deprives it of the power to propagate. Soviet communism, on the other hand, despite its ostensible commitment to materialism, has generated a body of ideas with a terrifying power to spread. And it is this impending defeat in the struggle to win adherents which will upset the balance and drive liberalism into loss of judgment and panic. One can almost say that this has now occurred. We see before us the paradox of materialist Russia expanding by the irresistible force of idea, while the United States, which supposedly has the heritage of values and ideals, frantically throws up barricades of money around the globe.

It will perhaps seem whimsical, but I have thought that the most promising bid for peace would be for the two great rivals to dispatch, each to the other, their ablest philosophers. Then we would see which side could convert the other with reference to the nature of the world and of man. And the world, having agreed in advance to abide by the decision, would thus be made one. This is the only hope for unity. The circumstance of living together in space and time has never yet made men peaceful. Rather, the contrary is true; and there are wise words by Hamilton in the *Federalist*: "It has from long observation of the progress of society become a sort of axiom in politics, that vicinity, or nearness of situation, constitutes nations natural enemies." The supposition that science is uniting the nations by bringing them closer together physically is but another aspect of a theory previously noted that natural means can take the place of creed as the binding element.

It is unlikely, therefore, that the era of soft living which our scientists and advertisers have promised will be realized on any condition. While these two worlds face each other there seems to remain only the question of whether the West will allow comfort to soften it to a point at which defeat is assured or whether it will accept the rule of hardness and discover means of discipline. If the latter course is chosen, it seems likely that the Western people are destined not for the happiness which they have promised themselves, but for something like Péguy's "socialist poverty." In an effort to secure themselves against the challenge of dynamism they will divert more of their substance and strength into armies and bureaucracies, the former to afford them protection from attack, the latter to effect internal order. In this event, personality will hardly survive. The individual will be told that the state is moving to guarantee his freedom, as in a sense it will be; but, to do so, it must prohibit individual indulgence and even responsibility. To give strength to its will, the state restricts the wills of its citizens. This is a general formula of political organization. All such questions lead inevitably to the question of discipline. The Russians with habitual clarity of purpose have made their choice; there is to be discipline, and it is to be enforced by the elite controlling the state. Now the significance of this for the West is that one choice is made for it too; there will be discipline here if the West is to survive. Organization always makes imperative counterorganization. A force in being is a threat to the unorganized, who must answer by becoming an organized force themselves. Thus a great decision confronting the West in the future is how to overcome the spoiled-child psychology sufficiently to discipline for struggle. (The attempt of the United States to make military service attractive by offering high pay, free college education, and other benefits looks suspiciously like bribing the child with candy.)

In these ways we get our reminders that science has not exempted us from struggle in life, though patterns change and deceive the shallow.

The failure of discipline in empirical societies can be traced to a warfare between the productive and the consumptive faculties. The spoiled child is simply one who has been allowed to believe that his consumptive faculty can prescribe the order of society. How an entire social group may fall victim to this may be illustrated by the development of collective bargaining. Demagogic leaders have told the common man that he is entitled to much more than he is getting; they have not told him the less pleasant truth that, unless there is to be expropriation—which in any case is only a temporary resource—the increase must come out of greater productivity. Now all productivity requires discipline and subordination; the simple endurance of toil requires control of passing desire. Here man is in a peculiar dilemma: the more he has of liberty, the less he can have of the fruits of productive work. The more he is spoiled, the more he resents control, and thus he actually defeats the measures which would make possible a greater consumption. "Undemocratic" productivity is attacked by "democratic" consumption; and, since there is no limit to appetite, there is no limit to the crippling of productive efficiency by the animal desire to consume, once it is in a position to make its force felt politically. Was there ever a more effective way to sabotage a nation's economy than to use the prestige of government to advocate the withholding of production? Strikes were originally regarded as conspiracies, and so they will have to be again when the free nations find collapse staring them in the face. What happens finally is that socialism, whose goal is materialism, meets the condition by turning authoritarian; that is to say, it is willing to institute control by dictation in order to raise living standards and not disappoint the consumptive soul. To the extent that socialism has done this by means of irrational appeals—and no others have been found efficacious in the long run—we have seen the establishment of fascist systems.

We need go no further to see why self-advertised leaders of the masses today, whether they owe their office to election or to coup d'état, have turned dictator. They have had to perceive that what the masses needed was a plan for harmony and for work. Now any plan, however arbitrary, will yield something better than chaos—this truth is merely a matter of definition. Accordingly, programs with fantastic objectives, some of them contradictory, have been set up. That they put an end temporarily to disorder and frustration is historical fact. A study of their motivation, however, shows that they all had scapegoats; they were against something. The psychology of this should not be mystifying; the spoiled child is aggrieved and wants redress. A course of action which keeps him occupied while allowing him to express his resentments seems perfect. We should recall the strange mélange of persons whom fascism cast in the role of villain: aristocrats, intellectuals, millionaires, members of racial minorities. In the United States there has been a similar tendency officially to castigate "economic royalists," managers of industry, "bourbons," and all who on any grounds could be considered privileged. It looks alarmingly like a dull hatred of every form of personal superiority. The spoiled children perceive correctly that the superior person is certain, sooner or later, to demand superior things of them, and this interferes with consumption and, above all, with thoughtlessness.

It is rather plain by now that even thrift is regarded as an evidence of such superiority. Regularly in the day of social disintegration there occur systematic attacks upon capital. Though capital may, on the one hand, be the result of unproductive activity—or of "theft," as left-wingers might declare—on the other hand, it may be the fruit of industry and foresight, of self-denial, or of some superiority of gifts. The attack upon capital is not necessarily an attack upon inequity. In the times which we describe it is likely to be born of love of ease, detestation of discipline, contempt for the past; for, after all, an accumulation of capital represents an extension of past effort into the present. But self-pampering, present-minded modern man looks neither before nor after; he marks inequalities of condition and, forbidden by his dogmas to admit inequalities of merit, moves to obliterate them. The outcry comes masked as an assertion that property rights should not be allowed to stand in the way of human rights, which would be well enough if human rights had not been divorced from duties. But as it is, the mass simply decides that it can get something without submitting to the discipline of work and proceeds to dispossess. Sir Flinders Petrie has written: "When democracy has attained full power, the majority without capital necessarily eat up the capital of the minority, and the civilization steadily decays." I would suggest as worth considering in this connection the difficulties of the Third Republic in maintaining the ideal of honest toil against the pressure of venality and politics and, on the other side, the ruthless determination of the Bolsheviks to permit no popular direction of affairs.

In the final analysis this society is like the spoiled child in its incapacity to think. Anyone can observe in the pampered children of the rich a kind of irresponsibility of the mental process. It occurs simply because they do not have to think to survive. They never have to feel that definition must be clear and deduction correct if they are to escape the sharp penalties of deprivation. Therefore the typical thinking of such people is fragmentary, discursive, and expressive of a sort of contempt for realities. Their conclusions are not "earned" in the sense of being logically valid but are seized in the face of facts. The young scion knows that, if he falls, there is a net below to catch him. Hardness of condition is wanting. Without work to do, especially without work that is related to our dearest aims, the mental sinews atrophy, as do the physical. There is evidence that the masses, spoiled by like conditions, incur a similar flabbiness and in crises will prove unable to think straight enough to save themselves.

This is, in conclusion, a story of weakness resulting from a false world picture. The withering-away of religious belief, the conviction that all fighting faiths are due to be supplanted, as Mr. Justice Holmes intimated in a decision, turn thoughts toward selfish economic advantage. The very attainment of this produces a softening; the softening prompts a search for yet easier ways of attaining the same advantage, and then follows decline. So long as private enterprise survives, there remain certain pressures not related to mass aspiration, but when industrial democracy insistently batters at private control, this means of organization and direction diminishes. Society eventually pauses before a fateful question: Where can it find a source of discipline?

7

The Last Metaphysical Right

In a country where the sole employer is the State, opposition means
death by slow starvation.

TROTSKY

The foregoing chapters have been concerned with various stages of
modern man's descent to chaos. Beginning with the first yielding to
materialism, we have seen a train of consequences proceeding, in
the same way that conclusions come from premises, to the egotism
and social anarchy of the present world. The topic now changes,
for the fact of one's writing signifies that he admits no necessity
for these things. The remaining chapters therefore present means
of restoration.

At the outset of proposing any reform we must ask for two
postulates, that man both can know and can will. Some may think
they are too doubtful to be assumed, but without them there is no
hope of recovery. In the confidence that those who have considered
these questions most deeply will agree that there is a presumption
in their favor, I shall proceed to outline the task of healing.

I have endeavored to make plain in every way that I regard all
the evils in our now extensive catalogue as flowing from a falsified
picture of the world which, for our immediate concern, results in an
inability to interpret current happenings. Hysterical optimism is a

sin against knowledge, and the conviction has been here expressed that nothing substantial can be done until we have brought sinners to repentance. Such phrases echo the language of a world thought past reviving, but the statement means simply that those who are in a quandary must be made to see that quandary. Complacency does not look before and after. It has been said with probable truth that the Roman Empire was in decline four hundred years before the situation was generally realized. The Whig theory of history, teaching that the most advanced point in time is the most advanced in development, is total abandonment of discrimination. Once man has regained sufficient humility to confess that ideals have been dishonored and that his condition is a reproach, one obstruction has been removed.

We must avoid, however, the temptation of trying to teach virtue directly, a dubious proceeding at any time and one under special handicaps in our age. It is necessary rather to seek out those "incalculably subtle powers" of which Ortega y Gasset speaks. This means that the beginning must not be less hardheaded and sophisticated than dozens of competing doctrines which would lure people into paths of materialism and pragmatism. Good will alone fails in the same way as does sentiment without the underpinning of metaphysic.

The first positive step must be a driving afresh of the wedge between the material and the transcendental. This is fundamental: without a dualism we should never find purchase for the pull upward, and all idealistic designs might as well be scuttled. I feel that this conclusion is the upshot of all that has here been rehearsed. That there is a world of ought, that the apparent does not exhaust the real—these are so essential to the very conception of improvement that it should be superfluous to mention them. The opening made by our wedge is simply a denial that whatever is, is right, which takes the form of an insistence upon the rightness of right. Upon this rock of metaphysical right we shall build our house. That the thing is not true and the act is not just unless these conform to a conceptual ideal—if we can make this plain again, utilitarianism and pragmatism will have been defeated. For such are the ultimates which determine value, significance, and even definition. Since knowledge finally depends on criteria of truth, we can even restore belief in the educative power of experience—which relativism and skepticism both deny. The prospect of living again in a world of metaphysical certitude—what relief will this not bring to those made seasick by the truth-denying doctrines of the relativists! To bring dualism back into the world and to rebuke the moral impotence fathered by empiricism is then the broad character of our objective.

Because we are now committed to a program which has practical applications, we must look for some rallying-point about which to organize. We face the fact that our side has been in retreat for four hundred years without, however, having been entirely driven from the field. One corner is yet left. When we survey the scene to find something which the rancorous leveling wind of utilitarianism has not brought down, we discover one institution, shaken somewhat, but still strong and perfectly clear in its implications. This is the right of private property, which is, in fact, the last metaphysical right remaining to us. The ordinances of religion, the prerogatives of sex and of vocation, all have been swept away by materialism, but the relationship of a man to his own has until the present largely escaped attack. The metaphysical right of religion went out at the time of the Reformation. Others have been gradually eroded by the rising rule of appetite. But the very circumstance that the middle class rose to power on property led it to consecrate property rights at the same time that it was liquidating others. Accordingly, private property was made one of the absolute rights of man by the middle-class French Revolution, and it was firmly guaranteed by all the "free" constitutions of the early nineteenth century. Its recognition by the American constitution was unequivocal.

Now that the middle class itself is threatened, the concept of private property loses defenders, but it is still with us, and, though we may not be happy about its provenance, here is a tool at hand. Its survival may be an accident, yet it expresses an idea. It is the sole thing left among us to illustrate what right, independent of service or utility, means.

We say the right of private property is metaphysical because it does not depend on any test of social usefulness. Property rests upon the idea of the *hisness* of *his: proprietas, Eigentum*, the very words assert an identification of owner and owned. Now the great value of this is that the fact of something's being private property removes it from the area of contention. In the *hisness* of property we have dogma; there discussion ends. Relativists from the social sciences, who wish to bring everyone under secular group control, find this an annoying impediment. But is it not, in truth, quite comforting to feel that we can enjoy one right which does not have to answer the sophistries of the world or rise and fall with the tide of opinion? The right to use property as something private is, as I shall show more fully later, a sanctuary. It is a self-justifying right, which until lately was not called upon to show in the forum how its "services" warranted its continuance in a state dedicated to collective well-being.

At this point I would make abundantly clear that the last metaphysical right offers nothing in defense of that kind of property brought into being by finance capitalism. Such property is, on the contrary, a violation of the very notion of *proprietas*. This amendment of the institution to suit the uses of commerce and technology has done more to threaten property than anything else yet conceived. For the abstract property of stocks and bonds, the legal ownership of enterprises never seen, actually destroy the connection between man and his substance without which metaphysical right becomes meaningless. Property in this sense becomes a fiction useful for exploitation and makes impossible the sanctification of work. The property which we defend as an anchorage keeps its identity with the individual.

Not only is this true, but the aggregation of vast properties under anonymous ownership is a constant invitation to further state direction of our lives and fortunes. For, when properties are vast and integrated, on a scale now frequently seen, it requires but a slight step to transfer them to state control. Indeed, it is a commonplace that the trend toward monopoly is a trend toward state ownership; and, if we continued the analysis further, we should discover that business develops a bureaucracy which can be quite easily merged with that of government. Large business organizations, moreover, have seldom been backward about petitioning government for assistance, since their claim to independence rests upon desire for profit rather than upon principle or the sense of honor. Big business and the rationalization of industry thus abet the evils we seek to overcome. Ownership through stock makes the property an autonomous unit, devoted to abstract ends, and the stockholder's area of responsibility is narrowed in the same way as is that of the specialized worker. Respecters of private property are really obligated to oppose much that is done today in the name of private enterprise, for corporate organization and monopoly are the very means whereby property is casting aside its privacy.

The moral solution is the distributive ownership of small properties. These take the form of independent farms, of local businesses, of homes owned by the occupants, where individual responsibility gives significance to prerogative over property. Such ownership provides a range of volition through which one can be a complete person, and it is the abridgment of this volition for which monopoly capitalism must be condemned along with communism.

The assertion is tantamount to saying that man has a birthright of responsibility. That responsibility cannot exist when this essential right can be invaded in the name of temporary social usefulness and extraneous compulsion can be substituted. Therefore we are bound to maintain that some rights begin with the beginning and that some sort of private connection with substance is one of them. Others, too, we hope to see recognized, but our present concern is to find one ultimate protection for what is done in the name of the private person.

It is not a little disquieting to realize that in private property there survives the last domain of privacy of any kind. Every other wall has been overthrown. Here a unique privacy remains because property has not been compelled to give a justification of the kind demanded by rationalists and calculators. It must be maintained that property rests on the prerational sentiments in that we desire it not merely because it "keeps the man up"—this would reduce to utilitarianism—but because somehow it is needed to help him express his being, his true or personal being. By some mystery of imprint and assimilation man becomes identified with his things, so that a forcible separation of the two seems like a breach in nature.

But as we lay our plans for restoration, we find practical advantages in its preservation, and, while these are not to be pleaded as its ultimate justification, they are of legitimate use. To combat the swirling forces of social collapse, we must have some form of entrenchment, and especially do we need sanctuary against pagan statism. For it is evident that, as society gravitates toward a monstrous functionalism, the very basis of recovery may be destroyed before counterforces can be deployed. Almost every trend of the day points to an identification of right with the purpose of the state and that, in turn, with the utilitarian greatest material happiness for the greatest number. In states which have unreservedly embraced this ideal, we have seen the very sources of protest extirpated. A functional unit operates best when it has the machine's one degree of freedom, and governors of the modern kind will not be so restrained by sentiment as to tolerate less than the maximum efficiency. The day of respect for the "loyal opposition" has gone with the day of the gentleman class. The plain truth is that believers in value are on the point of being engulfed completely, so that they cannot find means of continuance on any condition. In the past, revolutionary movements have frequently drawn strength from elements in the very society that they proposed to overthrow. Such opportunity came through the existence of a measure of liberty. In the monolithic police state which is the invention of our age, assisted as it is by technology, surveillance becomes complete. And when we add to these political fanaticism, which seems an outgrowth of our level of development, the picture grows terrifying.[1]

Shall we not declare that the thinking people of our day, who see the suicide in massness and who individually reprobate the crimes of parties and of states, must be spared their private areas as the early Christians were the catacombs? In seeking protection against an otherwise omnipotent state, the opposition must now fall back upon the metaphysical right of private property. Actually something of this kind is a custom of long standing in the West. We have not regarded our political leaders as playing for their heads. If they meet failure through sponsoring some unpopular measure, they return home to their bit of the world, and there they plant, or they sell their professional services, or they write for publication in a market not entirely dominated by politics. So Abraham Lincoln, after losing the voters' favor by opposing the Mexican War, returned to the practice of law.

Private right defending noble preference is what we wish to make possible by insisting that not all shall be dependents of the state. Thoreau, finding his freedom at Walden Pond, could speak boldly against government without suffering economic excommunication. Walt Whitman, having become a hireling of government in Washington, discovered that unorthodox utterance, even in poetry, led to severance from income. Even political parties, driven from power by demagoguery, can subsist and work in the hope that a return to reason will enable men of principle to make themselves felt again. Private property cannot without considerable perversion of present laws be taken from the dissenter, and here lies a barrier to *Gleichschaltung*.

Nothing is more certain than that whatever has to court public favor for its support will sooner or later be prostituted to utilitarian ends. The educational institutions of the United States afford a striking demonstration of this truth. Virtually without exception, liberal education, that is to say, education centered about ideas and ideals, has fared best in those institutions which draw their income from private sources. They have been able, despite limitations which donors have sought to lay upon them, to insist that education be not entirely a means of breadwinning. This means that they have been relatively free to promote pure knowledge and the training of the mind; they have afforded a last stand for "antisocial" studies like Latin and Greek. In state institutions, always at the mercy of elected bodies and of the public generally, and under obligation to show practical fruits for their expenditure of money, the movement toward specialism and vocationalism has been irresistible. They have never been able to say that they will do what they will with their own because their own is not private. It seems fair to say that the opposite of the private is the prostitute.

Not only does the citadel of private property make existence physically possible for the protestant; it also provides indispensable opportunity for training in virtue. Because virtue is a state of character concerned with choice, it flourishes only in the area of volition. Not until lately has this fundamental connection between private property and liberty been stressed; here in the domain of private property, rational freedom may prove the man; here he makes his virtue an active principle, breathing and exercising it, as Milton recommended. Without freedom, how is anyone to pass his probation? Consider Thoreau, or any hard-bitten New England farmer of Thoreau's day, beside the pitiful puling creature which statism promises to create. The comparison points to this: a great virtue is realizable here, but we must be willing to meet its price.

It may indeed appear before the struggle is over that the attack upon private property is but a further expression of the distrust of reason with which our age seems fatally stricken. When it is no longer believed that there is a restraining reason in accordance with which men may act, it follows that the state cannot permit individual centers of control. The repudiation of transcendentalism compels the state to believe that individual centers of control will be governed by pure egotism, as indeed they largely are at present. At the same time, this repudiation pushes aside the concept of inviolability. The modern state does not comprehend how anyone can be guided by something other than itself. In its eyes pluralism is treason. Once you credit man with the power of reason and with inviolable rights, you set bounds beyond which the will of majorities may not go. Therefore it is highly probable that, subconsciously or not, the current determination to diminish the area of inviolable freedom masks an attempt to treat man as a mere biological unit. For liberty and right reason go hand in hand, and it is impossible to impugn one without casting reflection on the other.

These are some benefits of property in our time of crisis. But in ordinary times, too, property shows itself a benevolent institution by encouraging certain virtues, notable among which is providence. I tread gingerly here, observing how close I have come to a subject of bourgeois veneration, yet I am inclined to think that there is something philosophic in the practice of providence; certainly there is in the theory. Providence requires just that awareness of past and future that our provincial in time, eager to limit everything to present sensory experience, is seeking to destroy. It is precisely because providence takes into account the nonpresent that it calls for the exercise of reason and imagination. That I reap now the reward of my past industry or sloth, that what I do today will be felt in that future now potential—these require a play of mind. The notion that the state somehow bears responsibility for the indigence of the aged is not far removed from that demoralizing supposition that the state is somehow responsible for the criminality of the criminal. I will not deny that the dislocations of capitalism afford some ground for the former. But that is another argument; the point here is that no society is healthful which tells its members to take no thought of the morrow because the state underwrites their future. The ability to cultivate providence, which I would interpret literally as foresight, is an opportunity to develop personal worth. A conviction that those who perform the prayer of labor may store up a compensation which cannot be appropriated by the improvident is the soundest incentive to virtuous industry. Where the opposite conviction prevails, where popular majorities may, on a plea of present need, override these rights earned by past effort, the tendency is for all persons to become politicians. In other words, they come to feel that manipulation is a greater source of reward than is production. This is the essence of corruption.

While we are looking at the moral influence of real property, let us observe, too, that it is the individual's surest protection against that form of dishonor called adulteration. If one surveys the economic history of the West for the past several centuries, he discovers not only a decline of craftsmanship but also a related phenomenon, a steady shrinkage in the value of money. This is a fact of gravest implication, for it indicates that nations do not live up to their bargains. Their promises to pay are simply not kept. What happens is something like this: The nation gets into a difficulty, perhaps through war; then, instead of getting out by means of sacrifice and self-denial, it chooses the easier way and dishonors its obligations. Popular governments, whose disrespect for points of reference we have underscored, are especially prone to these solutions. A familiar term for the process is inflation, but, whatever it may be called, it represents the payment of pledges with depreciated media. France has afforded some of the most instructive lessons in this evil. During the course of the Great Revolution, for example, it was determined to issue paper money based on the nation's vast holding in expropriated land. Despite this guaranty, the assignats declined at a dizzy rate. In August, 1795, the record shows, a gold louis bought 36 of them; in September, 48; in November, 104; in

December, 152; in February of 1796 it bought 288, and eventually the issue was repudiated. But in the meantime, according to one historian, there came upon the nation "the *obliteration of the idea of thrift.* In this mania for yielding to present enjoyment rather than providing for future comfort were the seeds of new growths of wretchedness; and luxury, senseless and extravagant, set in: this, too, spread as a fashion. To feed it, there came cheatery in the nation at large, and corruption among officials and persons holding trusts: while the men set such fashions in business, private and official, women like Madame Tallien set fashions of extravagance in dress and living that added to the incentives to corruption. Faith in moral considerations, or even in good impulses, yielded to general distrust. National honor was thought a fiction cherished only by enthusiasts. Patriotism was eaten out by cynicism."[2] In our own day we have seen the franc decline to a minor fraction of its former value after the first World War and to a minor fraction of that after the second.

Adulteration can, of course, be a useful political weapon, and one of the first steps taken by a recent reform administration in the United States was the inflation of currency. However much this may be defended as a means of meeting the particular contingency, the essential character of the act is not altered: values determined politically by governments under shortsighted popular control tend to depreciate. There is perhaps a sort of economic royalism in maintaining that the standard of value of today shall not be different from that of yesterday.

Now productive private property represents a kind of sanctuary against robbery through adulteration, for the individual getting his sustenance from property which bears his imprint and assimilation has a more real measure of value. And this enables him to predict with some degree of assurance or, in the broadest sense, to examine his life. It is important to distinguish between the security which means being taken care of, or freedom from want and fear—which would reduce man to an invertebrate—and stability, which gives nothing for nothing but which maintains a constant between effort and reward.

There is, moreover, a natural connection between the sense of honor and the personal relationship to property. As property becomes increasingly an abstraction and the sense of affinity fades, there sets in a strong temptation to adulterate behind a screen of anonymity. A Spanish proverb tells us with unhappy truthfulness that money and honor are seldom found in the same pocket. Under present conditions money becomes the anonymous cloak for wealth; telling us how much a man has no longer tells us what he has. In former times, when the honor of work had some hold upon us, it was the practice of a maker to give his name to the product, and pride of family was linked up with maintenance of quality. Whether it was New England ships or Pennsylvania iron or Virginia tobacco, the name of an individual usually stood behind what was offered publicly as a tacit assumption of responsibility. But, as finance capitalism grew and men and property separated, a significant change occurred in names: the new designations shed all connection with the individual and became "General," "Standard," "International," "American," which are, of course, masks. Behind these every sort of adulteration can be practiced, and no one is shamed, because no one is identified; and, in fact, no single person may be responsible.[3] Having a real name might require having a character, and character stands in the way of profit. The invented names have a kinship with the dishonest hyperboles of advertising.

Accordingly, one of the most common tricks of the masters of modern commerce is to buy up an honored name and then to cheapen the quality of the merchandise for which it stands. The names have been detached from the things and can be bought and sold. They were established by individuals who saw an ideal of perfection in the tasks they undertook, and they were willing to be judged by their fidelity. In this way does utility drive out the old-fashioned virtue of loyalty to an ideal, which is honor.

Accordingly, if we take into account all reasonable factors, it is by no means clear whether the world is growing richer or poorer. The idea that it could be growing poorer will of course be scouted by those fascinated by a multiplicity of gadgets, but we should ponder carefully what is meant by this steady withdrawal of quality. We who have just passed through a great war are familiar with the feeling that no matter how much we improve our wage, we never seem able to buy what we want; we pay and pay, and yet the essential quality that we seek eludes us. Such depreciation has occurred to a marked extent over the last thirty years and to a lesser extent for far longer. The world is being starved for value. We are being told bigger lies and we are being fed less—this is the substantial fact flowing from the degradation of the ideal. A genuine article of fine material, put together by that craftsmanship which is oblivious of time, is almost certain today to be in the super-luxury class, if indeed it is not already a museum exhibit. The genius of value seems to have taken wings along with the other essences which nominalists would deny.

A most eloquent example may be seen in the story of housing. A hundred years ago, more or less, when men built houses to live in themselves, they were constructing private property. The purpose was one to be honored, and they worked well, with an eye at least to the third generation. This is a simple instance of providence. One can see those dwellings today in quiet villages of New England and in remote places of the South, the honesty of the work that went into them reflected even in a grace of form. A century or a century and a half goes by, and they are both habitable and attractive. Let us look next at the modern age, in which houses are erected by anonymous builders for anonymous buyers with an eye to profit margins. A certain trickiness of design they often have, a few obeisances to the god comfort; but after twenty years they are falling apart. They were never private except in a specious sense; no one was really identified with them. Thus our spiritual impoverishment is followed by material impoverishment, in that we are increasingly deceived by surfaces. We lose in the most practical manner conceivable when we allow intension to be replaced by extension.

We must now get back to some general aspects of our problem and inquire whether the distributive ownership of real property might not correct a subversion of values which has been a scandal of the last century. I refer here simply to economic determinism. The fact that property broke away from this metaphysical relationship gave it a presumptive autonomy which played havoc with our thinking about the whole world. A consequence evident to everybody was the enthronement of economic man. The tendency of property under capitalism to aggregate lent powerful support to the notion that economic factors are ultimate determinants. Perhaps this was only an interpretation of surface phenomena; yet so many men became the pawns of corporate economic bodies that it seemed plausible to explain all human activity as product or by-product of the search for economic satisfactions. (We must not forget, too, that Darwinism was lurking in the background.) Politics, arts, everything, came under the rule; man was primarily a food- and shelter-finding animal, and whoever wished the final explanation of political organizations and cultural differences was advised to seek it in what really counted—the struggle for material accommodation. It came to be assumed that politics was a mere handmaiden of economics, and books describing the ancillary role of political belief were received as revelations. This was the supreme falsification by the bourgeois mentality.

People who live according to a falsified picture of the world sooner or later receive sharp blows, and the first of these came in the Great Depression. It is interesting to note the reversal of roles which this disruptive experience effected. For everywhere the crisis was met by putting economic activity under stern political direction or, in other words, by setting political authority over supposedly unchangeable economic law. Such action, incidentally, occurred in the United States and in Germany at almost the identical moment. This corrected the fallacy by which economics had broken loose from the metaphysical hierarchy and presumed an exclusiveness. It will stand as a true observation that this episode marked the end of economic man. The principle re-emerged that what is done with economic goods must be somehow related to man's destiny. And so the world picture as final determinant was partially reestablished.

The idea of metaphysical right subsumes property, and it is this idea that was lost to view in man's orientation away from transcendence. If material goods had been seen as something with a fixed place in the order of creation rather than as the ocean of being, on which man bobs about like a cork, the laws of economics would never have been postulated as the ordinances of all human life. But this again requires belief in nonmaterial existence.

It would be naïve to take an unmixed delight in the thought that politics has at length dethroned economics. The simplest meaning of the event, together with that of many others we have detailed, is that the world of 1789 has come to an end. There is a degree of comfort in knowing that we are not at the mercy of iron economic laws and that we can will the character of our wealth-getting activities. This could, in fact, be an important step toward rational freedom. But, under the present dispensation, the prospect of making politics the final arbiter is not without its terror. No thoughtful person can feel that we have found means of getting our political authority regularly into the hands of the wise. We have here something like the fallacy of humanism carried over into politics; our magistrates are, alas, human, all too human. Can we admire, or even trust a man who is merely the common denominator of all men? We have escaped one form of irrational domination only to be threatened by another which may prove more irresponsible— domination by the propertyless bureaucrat. I emphasize this in order to keep before us the question of how to preserve the spirit of obedience in a purely secular society.

It is by now reasonably plain that the frantic peoples of Europe thought their solution was to turn over their lives to unrestricted political control. By doing this, they found temporary amelioration and the illusion of future security. But the people into whose hands they allowed authority to fall were so selfish and so irrational that they exemplified power without wisdom. They did demonstrate that political dictation can end economic chaos; but this, after all, was technique. The question of what to do after the power of political control had been sensed found no reasonable answer. The leaders cultivated a political fanaticism, which had the result, as Emil Lederer has shown, of institutionalizing massness. We have already pointed to the antithesis of mass and society. A primary object of those who wish to restore society is the demassing of the masses, and in this the role of property is paramount.

Private property, in the sense we have defined it, is substance; in fact, it is something very much like the philosophic concept of substance. Now when we envision a society of responsible persons, we see them enjoying a range of free choice which is always expressed in relation to substance. I certainly concur with Péguy that the relationship between spirit and matter is one of the great mysteries, but I do not think that the mystery calls for the annihilation of matter. It is, on the contrary, important to keep substance in life, for a man's character emerges in the building and ordering of his house; it does not emerge in complaisance with state arrangement, and it is likely to be totally effaced by communistic organization. Substance has a part in bringing out that distinction which we have admitted to be good; it is somehow instrumental in man's probation.

The issue involves, finally, the question of freedom of the will, for private property is essential in any scheme which assumes that man has choice between better and worse. It is given him like the Garden of Eden, and up to now he seems guilty of a second forfeit of happiness. An abuse, however, does not stigmatize the thing abused. And, underlying all, there is for us in this critical battle against chaos the concept of inviolable right. We prize this instance because it is the opening for other transcendental conceptions. So long as there is a single breach in monism or pragmatism, the cause of values is not lost. It is likely—though this is not a question to be resolved by babes and sucklings—that human society cannot exist without some resource of sacredness. Those states which have sought openly to remove it have tended in the end to assume divinity themselves.

Therefore one inviolable right there must be to validate all other rights. Unless something exists from which we can start with moral certitude, we cannot depend on those deductions which are the framework of coherent behavior. I have read recently that a liberal is one who doubts his premises even when he is proceeding on them. This seems the very prescription for demoralization if not for insanity. And I think it true that the sort of metaphysical moral right we have outlined bears comparison with the a priori principles which we cannot doubt when we do our thinking.

The Greeks identified god with mind, and it will be found that every attack upon religion, or upon characteristic ideas inherited from religion, when its assumptions are laid bare, turns out to be an attack upon mind. Moral certitude gives the prior assurance of right sentiment. Intellectual integrity gives clarity to practice. There is some ultimate identification of goodness and truth, so that he who ignores or loses faith in the former can by no possible means save the latter.

For centuries now opportunism has encroached upon essential right until certitude has all but vanished. We are looking for a place where a successful stand may be made for the logos against modern barbarism. It seems that small-scale private property offers such an entrenchment, which is, of course, a place of defense. Yet offensive operations too must be undertaken.

8

The Power of the Word

The corruption of man is followed by the corruption of language.

EMERSON

After securing a place in the world from which to fight, we should turn our attention first to the matter of language. The impulse to dissolve everything into sensation has made powerful assaults against the forms which enable discourse, because these institute a discipline and operate through predications which are themselves fixities. We have sought an ultimate sanction for man's substance in metaphysics, and we must do the same for his language if we are to save it from a similar prostitution. All metaphysical community depends on the ability of men to understand one another.

At the beginning I should urge examining in all seriousness that ancient belief that a divine element is present in language. The feeling that to have power of language is to have control over things is deeply imbedded in the human mind. We see this in the way men gifted in speech are feared or admired; we see it in the potency ascribed to incantations, interdictions, and curses. We see it in the legal force given to oath or word. A man can bind himself in the face of contingencies by saying Yea or Nay, which can only mean that words in common human practice express something transcending the moment. Speech is, moreover, the vehicle of order, and those who command it are regarded as having superior insight, which must be into the necessary relationship of things. Such is the philosophic meaning of great myths. "And out of the ground the Lord God formed every beast of the field, and every fowl of the air; and brought them unto Adam to see what he would call them, and whatever Adam called every living creature, that was the name thereof." This story symbolizes the fact that man's overlordship begins with the naming of the world. Having named the animals, he has in a sense ordered them, and what other than a classified catalogue of names is a large part of natural science? To discover what a thing is "called" according to some system is the essential step in knowing, and to say that all education is learning to name rightly, as Adam named the animals, would assert an underlying truth. The sentence passed upon Babel confounded the learning of its builders.

As myth gives way to philosophy in the normal sequence we have noted, the tendency to see a principle of divinity in language endures. Thus we learn that in the late ancient world the Hebrew *memra* and the Greek *logos* merged, and in the Gospel of John we find an explicit identification:

In the beginning was the Word, and the Word was with God, and the Word was God.
The same was in the beginning with God.

A following verse declares that *logos* as god lies behind the design of the cosmos, for "without him was not anything made that was made." Speech begins to appear the principle of intelligibility. So when wisdom came to man in Christ, in continuation of this story, "the Word was made flesh and dwelt among us." The allegory need give no difficulty; knowledge of the prime reality comes to man through the word; the word is a sort of deliverance from the shifting world of appearances. The central teaching of the New Testament is that those who accept the word acquire wisdom and at the same time some identification with the eternal, usually figured as everlasting life.

It seems that man, except in periods of loss of confidence, when skepticism impugns the very possibility of knowledge, shows thus an incurable disposition to look upon the word as a means of insight into the noumenal world. The fact that language is suprapersonal, uniting countless minds which somehow stand in relationship to an overruling divinity, lies at the root of this concept. If, as Karl Vossler has observed, "Everything that is spoken on this globe in the course of ages must be thought of as a vast soliloquy spoken by the human mind, which unfolds itself in millions of persons and characters, and comes to itself again in their reunion," language must somehow express the enduring part. Certainly one of the most important revelations about a period comes in its theory of language, for that informs us whether language is viewed as a bridge to the noumenal or as a body of fictions convenient for grappling with transitory phenomena. Not without point is the cynical observation of Hobbes that "words are wise men's counters—they do but reckon by them—but they are the money of fools." Doctrines thus sharply defined can tell us whether a period is idealistic or pragmatic. Because this circumstance concerns the problem of restoration at a critical point, it becomes necessary to say something about contemporary theories of language.

The most notable development of our time in the province of language study is the heightened interest in semantics, which seems to stem from a realization that words, after all, have done things on their own, so to express it. I shall review briefly the state of the question. The problem of the word was argued with great acuteness by the Middle Ages, and one of the first major steps in the direction of modern skepticism came through the victory of Occam over Aquinas in a controversy about language. The statement that *modi essendi et subsistendi* were replaced by *modi significandi et intelligendi*, or that ontological referents were abandoned in favor of pragmatic significations, describes broadly the change in philosophy which continues to our time. From Occam to Bacon, from Bacon to Hobbes, and from Hobbes to contemporary semanticists, the progression is clear: ideas become psychological figments, and words become useful signs.

Semantics, which I shall treat as an extreme outgrowth of nominalism, seems inspired by two things: a feeling that language does not take into account the infinite particularity of the world and a phobia in the face of the autonomous power of words.

The semanticists are impressed with the world as process, and, feeling with Heraclitus that no man can step in the same river twice, they question how the fixities of language can represent a changeful reality. S. I. Hayakawa, one of the best-known popularizers of the subject, tells us that "the universe is in a perpetual state of flux."[1] Alfred Korzybski has declared that the use of the word "is," in the sense condemned in his system of semantics, so falsifies the world that it could endanger our sanity. Such men work laboriously to show by categories of referents all the things a single term can mean, and, at the same time, they take into account the circumstances of the user, apparently in an effort to correlate him with the world of becoming. (This should recall the earlier tendency of Romanticism to regard a work of art as expressive of the artist's emotional condition at the moment of its execution.) They desire language to reflect not conceptions of verities but qualities of perceptions, so that man may, by the pragmatic theory of success, live more successfully. To one completely committed to this realm of becoming, as are the empiricists, the claim to apprehend verities is a sign of psychopathology. Probably we have here but a highly sophisticated expression of the doctrine that ideals are hallucinations and that the only normal, sane person is the healthy extrovert, making instant, instinctive adjustments to the stimuli of the material world. To such people as these, Christ as preacher of the Word, is a "homosexual paranoiac." In effect, their doctrine seems part of the general impulse to remove all barriers to immediate apprehension of the sensory world, and so one must again call attention to a willingness to make the physical the sole determinant of what is.

In recognizing that words have power to define and to compel, the semanticists are actually testifying to the philosophic quality of language which is the source of their vexation. In an attempt to get rid of that quality, they are looking for some neutral means which will be a nonconductor of the current called "emotion" and its concomitant of evaluation. They are introducing into language, in the course of their prescriptions, exactly the same atomization which we have deplored in other fields. They are trying to strip words of all meaning that shows tendency, or they are trying to isolate language from the noumenal world by ridding speech of tropes.

Let us consider an illustration from Hayakawa's *Language in Action*, a work which has done much to put the new science before the public. It is easy to visualize a social situation, the author tells us, in which payment to unemployed persons will be termed by one group of citizens "relief" and by another "social insurance." One can admit the possibility, but what lies behind the difference in terminology? The answer is: a conception of ends which evaluates the tendency of the action named. The same sort of thing is encountered when one has to decide whether the struggle of the American colonists against Great Britain should be termed a "rebellion" or a "war for independence." In the first case, the bare existential thing, the payment of money to needy persons (and it will be noted that this translation does not purify the expression of tendency) is like anything else neutral as long as we consider it solely with reference to material and efficient causes. But, when we begin to think about what it represents in the totality, it takes on new attributes (emotional loading, these may be called) causing people to divide according to their sentiments or their metaphysical dream.

It is in such instances that the semanticists seem to react hysterically to the fear of words. Realizing that today human beings are in disagreement as never before and that words serve to polarize the conflicting positions, they propose an ending of polarity. I have mentioned, earlier, people who are so frightened over the existence of prejudice that they are at war with simple predication. The semanticists see in every epithet a prejudice.

The point at issue is explained by a fundamental proposition of Aquinas: "Every form is accompanied by an inclination." Now language is a system of forms, which both singly and collectively have this inclination or intention. The aim of semantics is to dissolve form and thereby destroy inclination in the belief that the result will enable a scientific manipulation. Our argument is that the removal of inclination destroys the essence of language.

Let us look more closely at the consequence of taking all tendentious meaning from speech. It is usually supposed that we would then have a scientific, objective vocabulary, which would square with the "real" world and so keep us from walking into stone walls or from fighting one another over things that have no existence. Actually the result would be to remove all teleology, for language would no no longer have *nisus*, and payment to the needy would be neither "relief" nor "social insurance" but something without character, which we would not know how to place in our scheme of values. (The fact that equalitarian democracy, to the extent that it makes leadership superfluous or impossible, is repudiating teleology must not be overlooked here. Teleology enjoins from above; equalitarian democracy takes its counsel without point of reference. The advantage of semantics to equalitarian democracy is pointed out by some semanticists.)

Hayakawa has said further that "arguments over intensional meaning can result only in irreconcilable conflict."[2] With the proper qualifications, this observation is true. Since language expresses tendency, and tendency has direction, those who differ over tendency can remain at harmony only in two ways: (1) by developing a complacency which makes possible the ignoring of contradictions and (2) by referring to first principles, which will finally re-

move the difference at the expense of one side. If truth exists and
is attainable by man, it is not to be expected that there will be
unison among those who have different degrees of it. This is one
of the painful conditions of existence which the bourgeoisie like
to shut from their sight. I see no reason to doubt that here is the
meaning of the verses in Scripture: "Suppose ye that I am come to
give peace on earth? I tell you, Nay; but rather division" and "I
bring not peace, but a sword." It was the mission of the prophet to
bring a metaphysical sword among men which has been dividing
them ever since, with a division that affirms value. But amid this
division there can be charity, and charity is more to be relied on to
prevent violence than are the political neofanaticisms of which our
age is signally productive. Positivism cannot grant theology's basis
of distinction, but neither can it provide a ground for charity.

When we look more narrowly at the epistemological problem
raised by the semanticists, we conclude that they wish to accept
patterns only from external reality. With many of them the notion
seems implicit that language is an illusion or a barrier between us
and what we must cope with. "Somewhere bedrock beneath words
must be reached," is a common theme. Some talk about achieving an infinite-valued orientation (this last would of course leave
both certitude and the idea of the good impossible). Mr. Thurman
Arnold, who seems to have assimilated most of the superficial doctrines of the day, takes a stand in the *Folklore of Capitalism* even
against definition. He argues that every writer on social institutions
"should try to choose words and illustrations which will arouse the
proper mental associations with his readers. If he doesn't succeed
with them, he should try others. If he is ever led into an attempt
at definition, he is lost." On the same footing of ingenuousness is
another observation in this work: "When men begin to examine
philosophies and principles as they examine atoms and electrons,
the road to the discovery of the means of social control is open."
The author of *Political Semantics*, fearful of the intervention of ab-
stractions, suggests that the reader, too, add something to the defi-

nition given, a notion savoring strongly of progressive education. "Possibly the reader himself should participate in the process of building up a definition. Instead of being presented with finished summary definitions he might first be introduced to an array of examples arranged in such a way as to suggest the 'mental picture' in terms of which the examples were chosen."[3] There is just enough here to suggest the Socratic method; but the true implication is that there are no real definitions; there are only the general pictures one arrives at after more or less induction. The entire process is but a climbing-down of the ladder of abstraction.

Now whether it is profitable to descend that ladder is certainly not a question to be begged. Semanticists imagine, apparently, that the descent is a way out of that falsity which universality imposes on all language. Do we know more definitely what a horse is when we are in a position to point to one than when we merely use the name "horse" in its generic significance? This concerns one of the most fundamental problems of philosophy—one on which we must take a stand; and I am ready to assert that we can never break out of the circle of language and seize the object barehanded, as it were, or without some ideational operation.

It must surely be granted that whatever is unique defies definition. Definition then must depend on some kind of analogical relationship of a thing with other things, and this can mean only that definition is ultimately circular. That is to say, if one begins defining a word with synonyms, he will, if he continues, eventually complete a circuit and arrive at the very terms with which he started. Suppose we allow Korzybski, who has been especially restive in what appears to him the imprisoning net of language, to testify from his experiments: "We begin by asking the 'meaning' of every word uttered, being satisfied for this purpose with the roughest definition; then we ask the 'meaning' of the words used in the definition, and this process is continued for no more than ten to fifteen minutes, until the victim begins to speak in circles as, for instance, defining 'space' by 'length' and 'length' by 'space.' When this stage is reached, we have usually come to the *undefined* terms of the given individual. If we still press, no matter how gently, for definitions, a most interesting fact occurs. Sooner or later, signs of affective disturbance appear. Often the face reddens; there is body restlessness—symptoms quite similar to those seen in a schoolboy who has forgotten his lessons, which he 'knows' but cannot tell. . . . Here we have reached the bottom and the foundation of all *non-elementalistic* meanings, the meanings of *undefined* terms, which we 'know' somehow but cannot tell."

Taking the experiment as Korzybski recounts it, I would wish to ask whether this schoolboy who has forgotten his lessons is not every man, whose knowledge comes by a process of recalling and who is embarrassed as by ignorance when he can no longer recall? He is here frustrated because he cannot find any further analogues to illustrate what he knows. Any person, it seems, can be driven back to that knowledge which comes to him by immediate apprehension, but the very fact of his possessing such knowledge makes him a participant in the communal mind. I do not desire to press the issue here, but I suspect that this is evidence supporting the doctrine of knowledge by recollection taught by Plato and the philosophers of the East. If we can never succeed in getting out of the circle of definition, is it not true that all conventional definitions are but reminders of what we already, in a way, possess? The thing we have never heard of is defined for us by the things we know; putting these together, we discover, or unbury, the concept which was there all the while. If, for example, a class in science is being informed that "ontogeny recapitulates phylogeny," it is only being asked to synthesize concepts already more or less familiar. Finding the meaning of the *definiendum* is finding what emerges naturally if our present concepts are put together in the right relation. Even empirical investigations of the learning process bear this out. Such conclusions lead to the threshold of a significant commitment: ultimate definition is, as Aristotle affirmed, a matter of intuition. Primordial conception is somehow in us; from this we proceed as already noted by analogy, or the process of finding resemblance to one thing in another.[4]

All this has bearing on our issue with semantics because words, each containing its universal, are our reminders of knowledge. For this reason it seems to me that semanticists are exactly wrong in regarding language as an obstruction or a series of pitfalls. Language, on the contrary, appears as a great storehouse of universal memory, or it may be said to serve as a net, not imprisoning us but supporting us and aiding us to get at a meaning beyond present meaning through the very fact that it embodies others' experiences. Words, because of their common currency, acquire a significance greater than can be imparted to them by a single user and greater than can be applied to a single situation. In this way the word is evocative of ideal aspects, which by our premises are the only aspects constituting knowledge. On this point I shall call as my witnesses two men as far apart as Shelley and a contemporary psychologist. The poet writes in *Prometheus Unbound*:

> Language is a perpetual Orphic song,
> Which rules with Daedal harmony the throng
> Of thoughts and forms, which else senseless and shapeless were.

Wilbur Marshall Urban declares in *Language and Reality*: "It is part of my general thesis that all meaning is ultimately linguistic and that although science, in the interests of purer notation and manipulation, may break through the husk of language, its non-linguistic symbols must again be translated back into natural language if intelligibility is to be possible."[5]

The community of language gives one access to significances at which he cannot otherwise arrive. To find a word is to find a meaning; to create a word is to find a single term for a meaning partially distributed in other words. Whoever may doubt that language has this power to evoke should try the experiment of thinking without words.

It has been necessary to make these observations because our subject is the restoration of language, and semantics has appeared to some a promising departure toward scientific reconstruction. In its seeking of objective determination, however, it turns out to represent a further flight from center. It endeavors to find the truth about reality in an agglomeration of peripheral meanings, as can be seen when its proponents insist on lowering the level of abstraction. This is only an attempt to substitute things for words, and, if words stand, in fact, for ideas, here is but the broadest aspect of our entire social disintegration. Here would be a vivid example of things in the saddle riding mankind. For the sake of memory, for the sake of logic—above all, for the sake of the unsentimental sentiment without which communities do not endure—this is a trend to be reversed. Those who regard the synthesizing power of language with horror are the atomists.

The opposition here indicated brings us necessarily to the important topic of symbolism. The attack upon the symbolic operations of language by positivists is only part of the general attack upon symbolism under way ever since it was widely agreed that there is but one world and that it is the world which is apparent to the senses. The logic is unexceptionable; since the symbol is a bridge to the other, the "ideational" world, those who wish to confine themselves to experience must oppose symbolism. In fact, the whole tendency of empiricism and democracy in speech, dress, and manners has been toward a plainness which is without symbolic significance. The power of symbolism is greatly feared by those who wish to expel from life all that is nonrational in the sense of being nonutilitarian, as witness the attack of Jacobins upon crowns, cassocks, and flags. As semanticists wish to plane the tropes off language, so do reformers of this persuasion wish to remove the superfluous from dress. It is worth recalling how the French Revolution simplified the dress of the Western world. At the time of this writing there appeared a report that during a leftist revolution in Bolivia the necktie was discarded as "a symbol of servility and conformity." The most tenacious in clinging to symbolic apparel have been the clerical and military callings, which we have already characterized as metaphysical; and now even the military service is under pressure to abandon its symbolic distinction in dress.

The same tendency is manifesting itself in the decay of honorifics. To the modern mind there is something so artificial and so offensive in titles of any kind that even "doctor" and "professor" are being dropped, though the military services cling grimly to their titles of rank. (There is a further lesson to be drawn from the fact that practitioners of the applied science of medicine have been allowed to keep theirs.) Honorifics are often mere flummery, to be sure, but one must not overlook the truth that they represent an effort to distinguish between men and men of parts. When not abused, they are an explicit recognition of distinction and hierarchy, a recognition that cannot be dispensed with where highly organized effort is required. The impulse to disorganize succeeds where it makes dress and language stand for just what is before us and not for transcendental attributes or past attainments—makes us see people in an instant of time, as does the camera.[6]

The well-known fondness of the Japanese for honorific expression is but an aspect of the highly symbolic character of their culture. Naturally, this symbolism became a target for those who imagined they should re-educate the Japanese. Nothing would give the West a more complete sense of victory over the East than the abolishment of its taboos and ritualistic behavior. In this light I think we are to understand a curious press dispatch of March, 1946, which declared that MacArthur's headquarters "had suggested to the Japanese motion picture industry that kissing scenes in the movies would be a step toward democratization." We have witnessed other attacks, inspired by good will and ignorance, upon the symbolic world picture of the Japanese, especially with reference to their religion and their emperor.

We return now to consider what is indicated by command over

the symbolistic power of language. It is, as even primitives know, a wonderful thing to have the gift of speech. For it is true historically that those who have shown the greatest subtlety with language have shown the greatest power to understand (this does not exclude Sophists, for Plato made the point that one must be able to see the truth accurately in order to judge one's distance from it if he is practicing deception). To take a contemporary example which has statistical support: American universities have found that with few exceptions students who display the greatest mastery of words, as evidenced by vocabulary tests and exercises in writing, make the best scholastic records regardless of the department of study they enter. For physics, for chemistry, for engineering—it matters not how superficially unrelated to language the branch of study may be—command of language will prognosticate aptitude. Facility with words bespeaks a capacity to learn relations and grasp concepts; it is a means of access to the complex reality.

Evidently it is the poet's unique command of language which gives him his ability to see the potencies in circumstances. He is the greatest teacher of cause and effect in human affairs; when Shelley declared that poets are the unacknowledged legislators of mankind, he merely signified that poets are the quickest to apprehend necessary truth. One cannot help thinking here of the peculiar fulness with which Yeats and Eliot—and, before them, Charles Péguy—foretold the present generation's leap into the abysm, and this while the falsehoods of optimism were being dinned into all ears. A poem of Eliot, "difficult" or "meaningless" in 1927, becomes today almost pat in its applications. The discourse of poetry is winged; the nominal legislators plod along empirically on foot. What can this mean except that the poet communes with the mind of the superperson? At the other extreme, those who confine their attention to the analysis of matter prove singularly inept when called upon to deal with social and political situations. If we should compile a list of those who have taught us most of what we ultimately need to know, I imagine that the scientists, for all the fanfare given them today, would occupy a rather humble place and that the dramatic poets would stand near the top.

It is difficult, therefore, to overrate the importance of skill in language. But for us there is the prior problem of preserving language itself; for, as the psyche deteriorates, language shows symptoms of malady, and today relativism, with its disbelief in truth, has made the inroads we have just surveyed upon communication. We live in an age that is frightened by the very idea of certitude, and one of its really disturbing outgrowths is the easy divorce between words and the conceptual realities which our right minds know they must stand for. This takes the form especially of looseness and exaggeration. Now exaggeration, it should be realized, is essentially a form of ignorance, one that allows and seems to justify distortion. And the psychopathic mind of war has greatly increased our addiction to this vice; indeed, during the struggle distortion became virtually the technique of reporting. A course of action, when taken by our side, was "courageous"; when taken by the enemy, "desperate"; a policy instituted by our command was "stern," or in a delectable euphemism which became popular, "rugged"; the same thing instituted by the enemy was "brutal." Seizure by military might when committed by the enemy was "conquest"; but, if committed by our side, it was "occupation" or even "liberation," so transposed did the poles become. Unity of spirit among our people was a sign of virtue; among the enemy it was a proof of incorrigible devotion to crime. The list could be prolonged indefinitely. And such always happens when men surrender to irrationality. It fell upon the Hellenic cities during the Peloponnesian War. Thucydides tells us in a vivid sentence that "the ordinary acceptation of words in their relation to things was changed as men thought fit."

Our situation would be sufficiently deplorable if such deterioration were confined to times of military conflict; but evidence piles up that fundamental intellectual integrity, once compromised, is slow and difficult of restoration. If one examines the strikingly different significations given to "democracy" and "freedom," he is forced to realize how far we are from that basis of understanding which is prerequisite to the healing of the world. To one group "democracy" means access to the franchise; to another it means economic equality administered by a dictatorship. Or consider the number of contradictory things which have been denominated Fascist. What has happened to the one world of meaning? It has been lost for want of definers. Teachers of the present order have not enough courage to be definers; lawmakers have not enough insight.

The truth is, as we have already seen, that our surrender to irrationality has been in progress for a long time, and we witness today a breakdown of communication not only between nations and groups within nations but also between successive generations. Sir Richard Livingstone has pointed out that the people of the Western world "do not know the meaning of certain words, which had been assumed to belong to the permanent vocabulary of mankind, certain ideals which, if ignored in practice under pressure, were accepted in theory. The least important of these words is Freedom. The most important are Justice, Mercy, and Truth. In the past we have slurred this revolution over as a difference in 'ideology.' In fact it is the greatest transformation that the world has undergone, since, in Palestine or Greece, these ideals came into being or at least were recognized as principles of conduct."[7] Drift and circumstance have been permitted to change language so that the father has difficulty in speaking to the son; he endeavors to speak, but he cannot make the realness of his experience evident to the child. This circumstance, as much as any other, lies behind the defeat of tradition. Progress makes father and child live in different worlds, and speech fails to provide a means to bridge them. The word is almost in limbo, where the positivists have wished to consign it.

Finally, we come to our practical undertaking. If empirical community avails nothing without the metaphysical community of language, the next step obviously is a rehabilitation of the word.

That is a task for education, and the remainder of this chapter will discuss a program by which we can, I venture to hope, restore power and stability to language.

Since man necessarily uses both the poetical and the logical resources of speech, he needs a twofold training. The first part must be devoted to literature and rhetoric, the second to logic and dialectic.

The order parallels our projected scheme of things. We have shown that sentiment is the ultimate bond of community, and this we wish to secure first of all. The young come to us creatures of imagination and strong affection; they want to feel, but they do not know how—that is to say, they do not know the right objects and the right measures. And it is entirely certain that if we leave them to the sort of education obtainable today from extra-scholastic sources, the great majority will be schooled in the two vices of sentimentality and brutality. Now great poetry, rightly interpreted, is the surest antidote to both of these. In contrast with journalists and others, the great poets relate the events of history to a pure or noble metaphysical dream, which our students will have all their lives as a protecting arch over their system of values. Of course, a great deal will depend on the character and quality of the instruction. At this point I would say emphatically that we do not propose to make students chant in unison, "Life is real, life is earnest, and the grave is not its goal," though it would not be unfortunate if many emerged with that feeling. There is a sentimental poetry, and it will have to be exposed (not censored, certainly; for to omit criticism of it would deprive us of our fairest chance to combat the sentimental rhetoric of the student's environment). There may be poetry vicious in nature, and that, too, will have to be taught for what it is. But opportunity to show the affective power of words and the profound illumination which may occur through metaphor is limitless.

Let us suppose that we have set our students to studying carefully a great unsentimental poem such as Andrew Marvell's *Ode*

on the Return of Cromwell from Ireland. This poem begins in a
mood of innocent lyricism and passes finally to a subtle debate
over the rival doctrines of revolution and legitimism. The student
can be brought to see its great compression of language, achieving
intense effects without exaggeration; then, perhaps, the evocation
of the character of Cromwell; and, last, an enduring problem of
man set in a historical context. All this is said with no implication
that the poem has a "message" in the banal sense. But, if we agree
that poetry is a form of knowledge, we must conclude that it does
teach something, and the foregoing is a catalogue of what a student
could conceivably get from one poem. Or consider the richness of
Shakespeare's plays and sonnets when they are intensively read or
the strange byways of sentiment—not all of them admirable, I will
grant—into which the modern poets may lead a sojourner.

In brief, the discipline of poetry may be expected first to teach
the evocative power of words, to introduce the student, if we may
so put it, to the mighty power of symbolism, and then to show him
that there are ways of feeling about things which are not provincial
either in space or time. Poetry offers the fairest hope of restoring
our lost unity of mind.

This part of his study should include, too, the foreign languages,
and, if we really intend business, this will mean Latin and Greek.
I will not list here the well-known advantages flowing from such
study, but I shall mention a single one which I think has been too
little regarded. Nothing so successfully discourages slovenliness in
the use of language as the practice of translation. Focusing upon
what a word means and then finding its just equivalent in another
language compels one to look and to think before he commits
himself to any expression. It is a discipline of exactness which used
to be reflected in oratory and even in journalism but which is now
growing as rare as considerate manners. Drill in exact translation
is an excellent way of disposing the mind against that looseness
and exaggeration with which the sensationalists have corrupted

our world. If schools of journalism knew their business, they would graduate no one who could not render the Greek poets.

In closing, let it be added that there is a close correlation between the growth of materialism and the expulsion of languages from curricula, which is a further demonstration that where things are exalted, words will be depressed.

Our next move toward rehabilitation is the study of Socratic dialectic. I do not place dialectic second on the assumption that it provides access to regions of higher truth; it seems more likely that the symbolism of poetry does this. But, since it is impossible for men to live without reason, we must regard this as their means of coping with the datum of the world after they have established their primary feeling toward it. The laws of reason, as Spinoza said, "do but pursue the true interest and preservation of mankind." We may therefore look upon training in dialectic as our practical regimen.

The most important fact about dialectic is that it involves the science of naming. The good dialectician has come to see the world as one of choices, and he has learned to avoid that trap fatal to so many in our day, the excluded middle. It is not for him a world of undenominated things which can be combined pragmatically into any pattern. From this failure to insist upon no compromise in definition and elimination come most of our confusions. Our feeling of not understanding the world and our sense of moral helplessness are to be laid directly to an extremely subversive campaign to weaken faith in all predication. Necessity for the logical correctness of names ceases to be recognized. Until the world perceives that "good" cannot be applied to a thing because it is our own, and "bad" to the same thing because it is another's, there is no prospect of realizing community. Dialectic comes to our aid as a method by which, after our assumptions have been made, we can put our house in order. I am certain that this is why Plato in the *Cratylus* calls the giver of names a lawgiver ($\nu o\mu o\theta\varepsilon\tau\eta s$); for a name, to employ his conception, is "an instrument of teaching and of distinguishing natures." But if we are to avoid confusion, the name-maker who is lawgiver cannot proceed without dialectic: "And the work of the legislator is to give names, and the dialectician must be his director if the names are to be rightly given." Plato sees here that name-giving and lawgiving are related means of effecting order. Actually stable laws require a stable vocabulary, for a principal part of every judicial process is definition, or decision about the correct name of an action. Thus the magistrates of a state have a duty to see that names are not irresponsibly changed.

In dialectic the student will get a training in definition which will compel him to see limitation and contradiction, the two things about which the philosophy of progress leaves him most confused. In effect, he will get training in thinking, whereas the best that he gets now is a vague admonition to think for himself.

Here, then, is a call for a fresh appreciation of language—perhaps, indeed, a respect for words as things. Here is an opening for education to do something more than make its customary appeal for "spiritual revival," which is itself an encouragement to diffuseness and aimlessness. If the world is to remain cosmos, we shall have to make some practical application of the law that in the beginning was the word.

9

Piety and Justice

Let parents, then, bequeath to their children not riches, but the spirit of reverence.

PLATO, *Laws*

The third and last stage of our journey back brings us within sight of the fair goal of justice. We have explained how man must establish himself in relation to property, and we have outlined a means to repair communication. We now approach a crowning concept which governs his attitude toward the totality of the world.

I realize the risk one incurs in using language associated with forces popularly discredited, but I see no way to sum up the offense of modern man except to say that he is impious. I shall endeavor to compensate by giving the word some rather concrete applications. First of all, I would maintain that modern man is a parricide. He has taken up arms against, and he has effectually slain, what former men have regarded with filial veneration. He has not been conscious of crime but has, on the contrary—and certainly this is nothing new to students of human behavior—regarded his action as a proof of virtue.

It is highly significant to learn that when Plato undertakes a discussion of the nature of piety and impiety, he chooses as interlocutor a young man who is actually bent upon parricide. Euthyphro,

a youth filled with arrogant knowledge and certain that he understands "what is dear to the gods," has come to Athens to prosecute
his father for murder. Struck by the originality of this proceeding,
Socrates questions him in the usual fashion. His conclusion is that
piety, which consists of co-operation with the gods in the kind of
order they have instituted, is part of the larger concept of justice. It
can be added that the outcome of the dialectic does not encourage
the prosecution. The implication is that Euthyphro has no right,
out of his partial and immature knowledge, to proceed contemptu-
ously against an ancient relationship.

In our contemporary setting the young man stands for science
and technology, and the father for the order of nature. For centuries now we have been told that our happiness requires an un-
relenting assault upon this order; dominion, conquest, triumph—
all these names have been used as if it were a military campaign.
Somehow the notion has been loosed that nature is hostile to man
or that her ways are offensive or slovenly, so that every step of
progress is measured by how far we have altered these. Nothing
short of a recovery of the ancient virtue of *pietas* can absolve man
from this sin.

The prevailing attitude toward nature is that form of heresy
which denies substance and, in so doing, denies the rightfulness of
creation. We have said—to the point of repletion, perhaps—that
man is not to take his patterns from nature; but neither is he to
waste himself in seeking to change her face. I do not think we have
a contradiction here, the desideratum being a sort of respectful
nonattachment.

The modern position seems only another manifestation of egotism, which develops when man has reached a point at which he
will no longer admit the right to existence of things not of his own
contriving. From somewhere in his self-centered being he brings
plans which he would truculently impose. The true religion, it is
said, is service to mankind; but this service seems to take the form
of securing for him an unconditional victory over nature. Now this

attitude is impious, for, as has been noted, it violates the belief that creation or nature is fundamentally good, that the ultimate reason for its laws is a mystery, and that acts of defiance such as are daily celebrated by the newspapers are subversive of cosmos. Obviously a degree of humility is required to accept this view.

On the other hand, it is the nature of unlimited egotism to deny any source of right ordering outside itself. It is a state of belligerence toward the nonself, and who will say that this is not the root of all those envies and aggrandizements which make people feel that today justice has departed from the world?

Piety is a discipline of the will through respect. It admits the right to exist of things larger than the ego, of things different from the ego. And, before we can bring harmony back into a world where now everything seems to meet "in mere oppugnancy," we shall have to regard with the spirit of piety three things: nature, our neighbors—by which I mean all other people—and the past. I propose to take these up in turn.

By nature I mean simply the substance of the world. It is a matter of elementary observation that nature reflects some kind of order which was here before our time and which, even after atomic fission, defies our effort at total comprehension. The wise student of her still says modestly with the soothsayer in *Antony and Cleopatra*, "In nature's infinite book of secrecy a little I can read." And the philosopher still maintains that substance, though open to abuse, is not in its nature evil. We are more successfully healed by the *vis medicatrix naturae* than by the most ingenious medical application. We get increasing evidence under the regime of science that to meddle with small parts of a machine of whose total design and purpose we are ignorant produces evil consequences. Thus "natural evil," put out the front door by science, re-enters at the back door, sometimes with renewed potency for harm. Triumphs against the natural order of living exact unforeseen payments. At the same time that man attempts to straighten a crooked nature, he is striving to annihilate space, which seems but another phase of the war against substance. We ignore the fact that space and matter are shock absorbers; the more we diminish them the more we reduce our privacy and security. Our planet is falling victim to a rigorism, so that what is done in any remote corner affects—nay, menaces—the whole. Resiliency and tolerance are lost. What an anxiety neurosis has the airplane brought into the world! With piety gone, every great invention proves shortsighted.

And here we must confront the paradox that this continual warring upon nature is not a sign of superiority to her; it is a proof of preoccupation with nature, of a sort of imprisonment by her. Thus the lion woos his bride! Those who endlessly try to subdue nature offer evidence that they are caught in the toils of her fascination. Spiritual people do not take nature for their bride, and, by paradox again, they are often the most successful lords of her. Perry Miller has claimed that the reason the Puritans of New England, intense religious zealots, achieved better than ordinary success in both war and business was that their doctrine taught them to cultivate a "deadness to the world." It was just this deadness to the world, a sort of distance from it, which left them freer and bolder to act than people sunk in materialism and the love of comfort. We have noted a similar analysis by De Tocqueville of religious-minded communities. This immersion in the task of reconstructing nature is an adolescent infatuation. The youth is an intellectual merely, a believer in ideas, who thinks that ideas can overcome the world. The mature man passes beyond intellectuality to wisdom; he believes in ideas, too, but life has taught him to be content to see them embodied, which is to see them under a sort of limitation. In other words, he has found that substance is a part of life, a part which is ineluctable. This humbler view of man's powers is the essence of piety; and it is, in the long run, more rewarding, for nature seems best dealt with when we respect her without allowing ourselves to want too fiercely to possess her.

It has been mentioned that the spoiled-child psychology is encountered almost solely in those people who have abandoned nature and who have signalized this abandonment by taking flight from country to city. Turn where we will, we find that the country-man has a superior philosophic resignation to the order of things. He is less agitated by the cycle of birth and death; he frets less; he is more stable in time of crisis. He is better integrated than his city cousin because he has piety enough to accept reality, which is possibly tantamount to a belief in providence. There seems much truth in the statement by Miller that after the Puritans had lost piety, they became "unable to face reality as unflinchingly as their forefathers." The result was that curious combination of optimism and moral impotence, discerned by students of New England culture from Vernon Parrington to John P. Marquand, which contrasts with the earlier pessimism and moral force.

Yet other peoples must say, "There but for the grace of God go I"; for this is a failure all are prone to. And this is why an essential step in retaining our hold upon the real reality is a definition of our proper relationship to nature. At one extreme is total immersion, which leaves man sentient but unreflective. At the other is total abstraction, which leads philosophically to denial of substance (this may be symbolized by flight to the city). The latter is the way of statistics and technology. The complete acceptance of nature and the complete repudiation of her turn out to be equally pernicious; we should seek a way of life which does not merge with her by responding to her every impulse, or become fatally entangled with her by attempting a complete violation. Either of these courses has the effect of making nature central to man's destiny, through force of attraction or repulsion. Santayana has observed that we should take leave of life as Ulysses took leave of Nausicaä, blessing it but not in love with it; and I think that our attitude toward physical nature should be similar. Thus we may say of the great material world that we do not desire it chiefly but that we think it has a place in the order of things which is entitled to respect.

The second form of piety accepts the substance of other beings. It is a matter of everyday observation that people of cultivation

and intellectual perceptiveness are quickest to admit a law of rightness in ways of living different from their own; they have mastered
the principle that being has a right qua being. Knowledge disciplines egotism so that one credits the reality of other selves. The
virtue of the splendid tradition of chivalry was that it took formal
cognizance of the right to existence not only of inferiors but also of
enemies. The modern formula of unconditional surrender—used
first against nature and then against peoples—impiously puts man
in the place of God by usurping unlimited right to dispose of the
lives of others. Chivalry was a most practical expression of the
basic brotherhood of man. But to have enough imagination to see
into other lives and enough piety to realize that their existence is a
part of beneficent creation is the very foundation of human community. There appear to be two types to whom this kind of charity
is unthinkable: the barbarian, who would destroy what is different
because it is different, and the neurotic, who always reaches out
for control of others, probably because his own integration has
been lost. However that may be, the shortsightedness which will
not grant substance to other people or other personalities is just
that intolerance which finds the different less worthy. The hope of
diminishing that spirit of fanaticism which threatens to rend our
world depends on this concession to the nonself. I find no sign that
those earnest souls who are today pleading for understanding see
this connection between tolerance and piety. Not until we have
admitted that personality, like nature, has an origin that we cannot
account for are we likely to desist from parricide and fratricide.

The third form of piety credits the past with substance. One
would think, from the frantic attempts made to cut ourselves off
from history, that we aspire to a condition of collective amnesia.
Let us pause long enough to remember that in so far as we are
creatures of reflection, we have only the past. The present is a line,
without width; the future only a screen in our minds on which
we project combinations of memory. In the interest of knowledge,
then, we have every reason to remember the past as fully as we can

and to realize that its continued existence in mind is positively a determinant of present actions. It has been well said that the chief trouble with the contemporary generation is that it has not read the minutes of the last meeting. Most modern people appear to resent the past and seek to deny its substance for either of two reasons: (1) it confuses them, or (2) it inhibits them. If it confuses them, they have not thought enough about it; if it inhibits them, we should look with a curious eye upon whatever schemes they have afoot. Imagination enables us to know that people of past generations lived and had their being amid circumstances just as solid as those surrounding us. And piety accepts them, their words and deeds, as part of the total reality, not to be ignored in any summing-up of experience. Are those who died heroes' and martyrs' deaths really dead? It is not an idle question. In a way, they live on as forces, helping to shape our dream of the world. The spirit of modern impiety would inter their memory with their bones and hope to create a new world out of good will and ignorance.

Awareness of the past is an antidote to both egotism and shallow optimism. It restrains optimism because it teaches us to be cautious about man's perfectibility and to put a sober estimate on schemes to renovate the species. What coursebook in vanity and ambition is to be compared with Plutarch's *Lives*? What more soundly rebukes the theory of automatic progress than the measured tread of Gibbon's *Decline and Fall*? The reader of history is chastened, and, as he closes his book, he may say, with Dante, in the *Inferno*: "I had not thought death had undone so many."

Among the Romans piety was considered a part of *aequitas*, which expressed the Platonic concept of justice, or the rendering to each his due. I have endeavored to show that something is due to nature, and to our fellow-men, and to those who have passed out of temporal existence. Modern civilization, having lost all sense of obligation, is brought up against the fact that it does not know what is due to anything; consequently its affirmations grow feebler. For this reason I wish to take up next certain forms of impiety which operate as disintegrating forces. I shall follow my order and deal first with an impiety toward nature.

I put forward here an instance which not only is typical of contempt for natural order but which also is of transcendent importance. This is the foolish and destructive notion of the "equality" of the sexes. What but a profound blacking-out of our conception of nature and purpose could have borne this fantasy? Here is a distinction of so basic a character that one might suppose the most frenetic modern would regard it as part of the *donnée* to be respected. What God hath made distinct, let not man confuse! But no, profound differences of this kind seem only a challenge to the busy renovators of nature. The rage for equality has so blinded the last hundred years that every effort has been made to obliterate the divergence in role, in conduct, and in dress. It has been assumed, clearly out of this same impiety, that because the mission of woman is biological in a broader way, it is less to be admired. Therefore the attempt has been to masculinize women. (Has anyone heard arguments that the male should strive to imitate the female in anything?) A social subversion of the most spectacular kind has resulted. Today, in addition to lost generations, we have a self-pitying, lost sex.

There is a social history to this. At the source of the disorder there lies, I must repeat, an impiety toward nature, but we have seen how, when a perverse decision has been made, material factors begin to exert a disproportionate effect. Woman has increasingly gone into the world as an economic "equal" and therefore competitor of man (once again equality destroys fraternity). But a superficial explanation through economic changes is to be avoided. The economic cause is a cause that has a cause. The ultimate reason lies in the world picture, for once woman has been degraded in that picture—and putting her on a level with the male is more truly a degradation than an elevation—she is more at the mercy of economic circumstances. If we say that woman is identical with man except in that small matter of division of labor in the procreation of the species, which the most rabid egalitarian is driven to accept, there is no reason why she should not do man's work (and by extension, there is no reason why she should not be bombed along with him). So hordes of women have gone into industry and business, where the vast majority of them labor without heart and without incentive. Conscious of their displacement, they see no ideal in the task. And, in fact, they are not treated as equals; they have been made the victims of a transparent deception. Taken from a natural sphere in which they are superior, they are set to wandering between two worlds. Women can neither have the prestige of the former nor, for the fact of stubborn nature, find a real standing in the latter.

So we began to see them, these *homunculae* of modern industrial society, swarming at evening from factories and insurance offices, going home, like the typist in *The Waste Land*, to lay out their food in tins. At length, amid the marvelous confusion of values attendant upon the second World War, came the lady marine and the female armaments worker. It is as if the centripetal power of society had ceased. What is needed at center now drifts toward the outer edge. A social seduction of the female sex has occurred on a vast scale. And the men responsible for this seduction have been the white-slavers of business who traffic in the low wages of these creatures, the executives, the specialists in "reduction of labor costs"—the very economists and calculators whose emergence Burke predicted for us.

The anomalous phase of the situation is that the women themselves have not been more concerned to retrieve the mistake. Woman would seem to be the natural ally in any campaign to reverse this trend; in fact, it is alarming to think that her powerfully anchored defenses have not better withstood the tide of demoralization. With her superior closeness to nature, her intuitive realism, her unfailing ability to detect the sophistry in mere intellectuality, how was she ever cozened into the mistake of going modern? Perhaps it was the decay of chivalry in men that proved too much.

After the gentleman went, the lady had to go too. No longer protected, the woman now has her career, in which she makes a drab pilgrimage from two-room apartment to job to divorce court.

Women of the world's *ancien régime* were practitioners of *Real politik* in this respect: they knew where the power lies. (One wonders what Queen Elizabeth would have said had feminist agitators appeared during her reign over England's green and pleasant isle.) They knew it lies in loyalty to what they are and not in imitativeness, exhibitionism, and cheap bids for attention. Well was it said that he who leaves his proper sphere shows that he is ignorant both of that which he quits and that which he enters. Women have been misled by the philosophy of activism into forgetting that for them, as custodians of the values, it is better to "be" than to "do." Maternity, after all, as Walt Whitman noted, is "an emblematical attribute."

If our society were minded to move resolutely toward an ideal, its women would find little appeal, I am sure, in lives of machine-tending and money-handling. And this is so just because woman will regain her superiority when again she finds privacy in the home and becomes, as it were, a priestess radiating the power of proper sentiment. Her life at its best is a ceremony. When William Butler Yeats in "A Prayer for My Daughter" says, "Let her think opinions are accursed,"[1] he indicts the modern displaced female, the nervous, hysterical, frustrated, unhappy female, who has lost all queenliness and obtained nothing.

What has this act of impiety brought us except, in the mordant phrase of Henry James's *The Bostonians*, an era of "long-haired men and short-haired women"?

Next, we must consider a form of impiety toward people which generally goes by the name of loss of respect for individuality. I do not think individuality a fortunate word for this conception because it signifies a cutting-off or separation, and crimes can be committed in that name. A more accurate designation would be personality, for this recognizes the irreducible character in every person and at the same time permits the idea of community.

Personality in its true definition is theomorphic. Individuality, on the other hand, may be mere eccentricity or perverseness. Individualism, with its connotation of irresponsibility, is a direct invitation to selfishness, and all that this treatise has censured can be traced in some way to individualist mentality. But personality is that little private area of selfhood in which the person is at once conscious of his relationship to the transcendental and the living community. He is a particular vessel, but he carries some part of the universal mind. Once again it happens that when we seek to define "the final worth of the individual," as a modern phrase has it, we find that we can reverence the spirit in man but not the spirit of man. The latter supposition was the fallacy of literary humanism. There is piety in the belief that personality, like the earth we tread on, is something given us.

It would be tedious to point out that rationalism and the machine are overwhelmingly against personality. The first is suspicious of its transcendental origin, and the second finds that personality and mechanism positively do not mix. Accordingly, the determination of our day to make all things uniform and all things public cannot forgive this last citadel of privacy. Since, after all, personality is the beginning of distinction, every figure in modern public life feels called upon to stress the regularity of his background, his habits, his aspirations. The contempt with which modern dictatorships and bureaucracies reject difference and dissent is but a brutal aspect of the same thing. Deviation from the proletarian norm bids fair to become the heresy of the future, and from this heresy there will be no court of appeal.

The plea for piety asks only that we admit the right to self-ordering of the substance of other beings. Unless this little point is granted, it is futile to talk of tolerance on a grander scale.

The most vocal part of modern impiety is the freely expressed contempt for the past. The habit is to look upon history in the same way that we look upon nature, as an unfortunate inheritance, and we struggle with equal determination to free ourselves from each. More specifically, this tendency appears in our effort to base institutions more and more on free speculation, which gives reason opportunity to expel sentiment. Now we have paid sufficient tribute to reason, but we have also insisted that the area of its profitable operation is an island in a sea of prerational sentiment. There is something to be said for George Fitzhugh's statement that "philosophy will blow up any government that is founded on it," if by philosophy we mean a purely formal inquiry into human institutions. The great proliferation of social science today seems to spring from just this fallacy; they provide us with rationales, but they are actually contemptuous of history, which gives us the three-dimensional experience of mankind. Empiricism finds it necessary to say, too, that history has not taught anything finally, for if it had, the time of trial and error would be over. But if past history has not taught anything, how will present history or future experiment?

A *pietas* toward history acknowledges that past events have not happened without law.

We must not overlook the fact that in the vocabulary of modernism, "pious" is a term of reproach or ridicule. A survey will show that it is always applied to persons who have accepted a dispensation. Now modernism encourages the exact opposite of this, which is rebelliousness; and rebellion, as the legend of the Fall tells us, comes from pride. Pride and impatience, these are the ingredients of that contumely which denies substance because substance stands in the way. Hence the war against nature, against other men, against the past. For modern man there is no providence, because it would imply a wisdom superior to his and a relationship of means to ends which he cannot find out. Instead of feeling grateful that some things are past his discovering (how odd it sounded when Churchill, the last survivor of the old school, declared that the secret of atomic power had been "mercifully withheld" from man), he is vexed and promises himself that one day the last arcanum will be forced to yield its secret.

His pride reveals itself in impatience, which is an unwillingness to bear the pain of discipline. The physical world is a complex of imposed conditions; when these thwart immediate expressions of his will, he becomes angry and asserts that there should be no obstruction of his wishes. In effect this becomes a deification of his own will; man is not making himself like a god but is taking himself as he is and putting himself in the place of God. Of this we have seen many instances.

He is unwilling to admit the condition of time, and to this may be attributed not only the growing indifference to quality but also the decay of style in all departments of contemporary life. For, regardless of how it is expressed, style is a sort of regulated movement which depends on the observing of intervals. This is true in manners as in music, both of which on the popular level have been collapsed by impatience. All style whatever formalizes that in which it occurs, and we have seen how the modern temper feels imprisoned by all form. Style and grace are never seen in those who have not learned the lesson of endurance—which is a version of the lesson of heroism.

When we ask modern man to accept the substance of nature and of history, we ask him, in a way, to harden himself. He must not, like the child, expect all delights freely; he must not, like the miseducated adult, expect all paradoxes to be resolved for him. He must be ready to say at times with Thomas Hooker: "The point is difficult and the mystery great." And as he learns that he is a creature who does not fully comprehend his creation, it is to be hoped that he will exercise caution in the appropriation of efficient means. His picture of the world will be changed profoundly if he merely has to take cognizance of the fact that he is dependent on the universe, as it in turn seems dependent on something else.

Here we return for the last time to the problem which loomed at the beginning of our discourse: the quest for true knowledge. With ignorance virtually institutionalized, how can we get man to see? Bewildered by his curious alienation from reality, he is unable to prescribe for himself, for he imagines that what he needs is more of the disease.

At this point I must pause long enough to say that the numerous people maintaining that we suffer only from a cultural lag, that man's spiritual progress has not caught up with his material progress, proceed on a completely misleading analogy. There is nothing to indicate that these two are complementary or that they can go forward on parallel tracks. It would be far truer to say that moral purpose is deflected by proximity of great material means as rays of light are bent by matter. The advocates of spiritual revival exhibit a weakness typical of liberalism in their unwillingness to recognize this opposition.

Thus present-day reformers combat dilution by diluting further, dispersion by a more vigorous dispersing. Now that we have unchained forces of unpredictable magnitude, all that keeps the world from chaos are certain patterns, ill understood and surviving through force of inertia. Once these disappear, and we lack even an adventitious basis for unity, nothing separates us from the fifth century A.D.

It is said that physicians sometimes ask patients, "Do you really wish to get well?" And, to be perfectly realistic in this matter, we must put the question of whether modern civilization wishes to survive. One can detect signs of suicidal impulse; one feels at times that the modern world is calling for madder music and for stronger wine, is craving some delirium which will take it completely away from reality. One is made to think of Kierkegaard's figure of spectators in the theater, who applaud the announcement and repeated announcement that the building is on fire.

I have tried, as far as possible, to express the thought of this essay in secular language, but there are points where it has proved impossible to dispense with appeal to religion. And I think this term must be invoked to describe the strongest sustaining power in a life which is from limited points of view "solitary, poor, nasty, brutish, and short." It can be shown in every case that loss of belief results in some form of bitterness. Ancient cynicism, skepticism, and even stoicism, which were products of the decline of Greek religion, each concealed a bitterness. There is bitterness in the thought that there may be no hell; for—in the irrefutable syllogism of the theologians—if there is no hell, there is no justice. And bitterness is always an incentive to self-destruction. When it becomes evident that the world's rewards are not adequate to the world's pain, and when the possibility of other reward is denied, simple calculation demands the ending of all. The task is how to keep men from feeling desperately unrewarded. Do they today wish to go on living, or do they wish to destroy the world? Some are unable to comprehend the depth of bitterness which may induce a desire for the second course.

Suppose we get an affirmative answer to our first question; people tell us they do want to go on living—and not just biologically as rats in the corners of wrecked cities but in communities of civilization. Then we must ask the question whether they are willing to pay the price. For possibly their attitude toward this is like their attitude toward peace: they want it, but not at the expense of giving up this and that thing which they have come to think of as the warp and woof of their existence.

There is an unforgettable scene in Lincoln Steffens' *Autobiography* which tells of a proposal made by Clemenceau at the Versailles Peace Conference. The astute Frenchman, having listened to much talk that this was a war to end war forever, asked Wilson, Lloyd George, and Orlando whether they were taking the idea seriously. After obtaining assent from each of the somewhat nonplussed heads of state, Clemenceau proceeded to add up before them the cost. The British would have to give up their colonial system; the Americans would have to get out of the Philippines, to keep their hands off Mexico; and on and on it went. Clemenceau's colleagues soon made it plain that this was not at all what they had in mind, whereupon the French realist bluntly told them that they wanted not peace but war. Such is the position of all who urge justice but really want, and actually choose, other things.

In the same way, we have to inform the multitude that restoration comes at a price. Suppose we give them an intimation of the cost through a series of questions. Are you ready, we must ask them, to grant that the law of reward is inflexible and that one cannot, by cunning or through complaints, obtain more than he puts in? Are you prepared to see that comfort may be a seduction and that the fetish of material prosperity will have to be pushed aside in favor of some sterner ideal? Do you see the necessity of accepting duties before you begin to talk of freedoms? These things will be very hard; they will call for deep reformation. It may well be that the course of degeneration has proved so enervating that there is no way of reinspiring with ideals. We know that such is often the case with individual histories.

Yet it is the duty of those who can foresee the end of a saturnalia to make their counsel known. Nothing is more certain than that we are all in this together. Practically, no one can stand aside from a sweep as deep and broad as the decline of a civilization. If the thinkers of our time cannot catch the imagination of the world to the point of effecting some profound transformation, they must succumb with it. There will be little joy in the hour when they can say, "I told you so." And their present efforts show small sign of effect. Perhaps we shall have to learn the truth along some *via dolorosa.*

It may be that we are awaiting a great change, that the sins of the fathers are going to be visited upon the generations until the reality of evil is again brought home and there comes some passionate reaction, like that which flowered in the chivalry and spirituality of the Middle Ages. If such is the most we can hope for, something toward that revival may be prepared by acts of thought and volition in this waning day of the West.

HOW *IDEAS HAVE CONSEQUENCES* CAME TO BE WRITTEN

By Ted J. Smith III

On February 16, 1948, the University of Chicago Press released for sale a slim new book with the deceptively bland title *Ideas Have Consequences*. The event was preceded and followed by a massive, two-pronged marketing campaign, one of the largest ever mounted by the Press. It had begun two months earlier when major bookdealers throughout the country were sent a letter announcing the book's publication. This was followed in early January with a letter and sheets of talking points to "key publicity persons" and telegrams to "key dealers."[1] Next came a full-page advertisement in the January 17 issue of the leading trade journal, *Publishers' Weekly*, which announced: "We are starting with $7,500 to advertise one of the most important books we have ever published" and offered 100 advance reading copies to "anyone in bookselling" who requested one.[2] On January 22, Press director William Terry Couch dispatched a letter to book review editors in which he compared *Ideas Have Consequences* to Friedrich Hayek's *The Road to Serfdom*. The American edition of Hayek's foundational critique of socialism had generated enormous controversy—and commensurate sales—when it was published by the Press in 1944, and Couch predicted a similar outcome for the new book. As he noted:

Well, we have another author, a professor, who has written another
book that violates the union rules. The title of the book is, *Ideas Have
Consequences*. The professor is Richard M. Weaver of the college [*sic*]
of the University of Chicago. You may expect to hear him and us in the
next few weeks called stupid, ignorant, reactionary and wicked, etc.
You may also hear others say the opposite—we expect so—but we
don't govern our publishing by the prospects for applause.[3]

By all indications, the initial phase of the campaign had its desired effect. Another full-page advertisement in the February 21
issue of *Publishers' Weekly* announced: "1st printing exhausted
three weeks before publication; 2nd large printing on the way."[4] It
is also clear that at least some major dealers took pains to promote
the book. For example, Marshall Field and Company in down-
town Chicago featured it in a spotlighted display at the main en-
trance to the book department. As described by the Press' sales
manager, Donald Barnes, the display had a "surrealist" theme,
and he called attention to "the use of polished driftwood and root-
knots, the tattered copper screening and the very, very daliesque
shadow frame portraying modern man in awful misery."[5]

For those familiar with the actual contents of *Ideas Have Consequences*, the use of a "surrealist" display featuring a "daliesque
shadow frame" to promote the book may seem somewhat strange.
But it was very much in keeping with the general tone and content
of the massive advertising campaign that immediately followed its
publication. The campaign was based initially on two full-page
advertisements which appeared in most of the major literary periodicals of the day, including *The Atlantic Monthly, The Chicago
Sunday Tribune Magazine of Books, Christian Century, The Nation, The New Republic, New York Herald Tribune Book Review,
The New York Times Book Review*, and *The Saturday Review of
Literature*. Both of the advertisements were illustrated with an image of the book in its dust jacket, and one emphasized elements
of the dust jacket design in its main visual. The dust jacket itself

was executed in shades of bright orange and light grey, peppered with a dense scattering of ragged, black and white newspaper headlines and leads such as "11th Red Veto Jolts U.N.," "Riot Torn India Free Today," "Jail 1,000 Strikers," and "Girl Delinquency Found Increasing." Stark, ugly, and modernistic, it conveys a sense of strident insistence which was faithfully echoed in the ads. One blared: "A calm, quiet, courageous book! A shocking, infuriating, revolutionary book! It may shatter your strongest convictions!" The other demanded to know: "If you believe our civilization is the most advanced in history—How do you explain these headlines?"[6]

It would be a serious understatement to say that the author was displeased with these efforts. As he noted in a letter to Robert Heilman:

> The dustjacket is an atrocity, and I still shudder every time I see it. My first impulse was to strip it off all the copies I sent my friends and write a note of explanation. How they ever thought that such a thing was suitable for a work of this content is more than I can guess.

He was also less than pleased with the expensive full-page advertisements, as indicated by his comments about one of them to Heilman:

> I don't know whether you saw one of these, but it was a sensationalistic, atom-bombshell affair, the very thing to draw a negative reaction from an already high-pressured public. As one of my colleagues remarked all too truly, it reminded one of advertisements of prophylactics.[7]

He was equally pointed in a comment to Cleanth Brooks:

> I cannot avoid a certain feeling of frustration over my dealings with the Press. I think that I handed them a piece of philosophy, and they have done everything in their power to present it as a piece of journalism.[8]

Despite these shortcomings, the promotional campaign did achieve at least some of its goals. Advance sales were excellent and a great deal of discussion was generated, as indicated in particular by the publication of more than 100 reviews of the book. As anticipated, however, the reviews were decidedly mixed in tone: those in regional newspapers and religious periodicals were generally quite favorable, while those in organs of the liberal establishment tended to sneering vituperation. The most damaging were a review by Howard Mumford Jones in the February 22 issue of *The New York Times Book Review*, which characterized the book as "irresponsible," and an essay by Dixon Wecter in the April 10 issue of *The Saturday Review of Literature*, which began with an attack on Robert Maynard Hutchins and his efforts at Chicago and ended by holding up *Ideas Have Consequences* as an emblem of the university's deficiencies. The reaction to the latter on the University of Chicago campus was particularly strong, and for a time Weaver had serious doubts about whether he would be able to keep his job. He described the reaction to the Wecter review in a letter to Cleanth Brooks:

> It created a great sensation here, and the bookstore had to order additional copies of this issue. To say that I became a marked man after this is to use the language of understatement. Murmurs began to be heard that the book should never have been published at all because it was unfairly taken to represent the philosophy of the University of Chicago. . . . R. S. Crane [chairman of the English Department] was irritated by the book from the outset, and since the appearance of Wecter's piece, in which the English department here was branded "bush league," he has been infuriated with me. We no longer speak.[9]

The fact that Weaver was concerned about his job calls attention to the truly extraordinary character of these events. At the time *Ideas Have Consequences* was published, Richard Weaver was a young man of 37, just five years out of graduate school and with a total of only eight published essays and book reviews to his credit. Although a faculty member at a highly prestigious university, he held only a one-year appointment as an instructor in the undergraduate College, where his principal assignment was to teach the freshman-level course in English composition. Because they were evaluated primarily on their performance in the classroom, there was little time or incentive for members of the College faculty to engage in any extensive program of research and publication, and few in fact did. For someone in Weaver's position to produce a book offering a sweeping indictment of the entire course of Western civilization over the past 500 years and a trenchant critique of the core values of modern American society is indicative, at the least, of a very advanced level of audacity. And for a major university press to place its full resources and reputation behind such a book is exceptional almost to the point of uniqueness. It is therefore worthwhile to inquire just how the book came into being.

At the most basic level of analysis it is clear that *Ideas Have Consequences* was the product of two somewhat independent strands in Weaver's thinking. The first of these has roots so deep in Weaver's intellectual development that it will be useful to sketch the course of his career up to the time when the idea for the book was first suggested to him.

Richard Malcolm Weaver was born in Asheville, North Carolina, on March 3, 1910, the first of four children of Richard M. "Dick" Weaver and Carrye (later "Carrie") Lee Embry Weaver. Dick Weaver, a popular and outgoing local businessman, was the junior partner in Chambers & Weaver, a successful livery stable and automobile agency. Carrye Weaver was born in Fayette County, Kentucky, but spent most of her adult life in nearby Lexington. In 1902, at the age of 28, she founded Embry & Co., a successful millinery shop which her brother William eventually expanded into one of the leading department stores in the city. Dick and Carrye met in 1907 and were married in November of the following year. It was his second marriage, her first.[10]

On December 16, 1915, Dick Weaver retired to bed early complaining of dizziness. A few hours later he was dead, the victim of a stroke at the age of 45.[11] His widow and children remained in North Carolina for a year or two, but she then moved the family to Lexington, where she opened a new millinery shop in direct competition with Embry & Co. That venture soon failed, however, and Carrye was forced to seek employment in her brother's store, where she worked as buyer and manager of the millinery department until her retirement in about 1939.[12]

Little is known about Richard Weaver's early education. In North Carolina, he apparently attended classes at a tiny private school conducted in one room of the teacher's home.[13] After his family moved to Lexington, he enrolled as a third grade student in a public elementary school a few blocks from his home. But he did not return the following year and it seems likely that he attended classes through the eighth grade at some private school in the Lexington area.[14]

The record of Weaver's education becomes more detailed after September 1924, when he enrolled as a freshman in the Academy of Lincoln Memorial University in Harrogate, Tennessee. By all accounts, he was an unusually serious and high-minded student who displayed a marked interest in moral and philosophical issues. In November 1925 he joined with Vadus Carmack—a fellow student in the Academy—and William Maury Mitchell—a student in the University, four years his senior, who was to become Weaver's lifelong friend—to form the Societas Philosophiae Scientiaeque. The purpose of the society, which met each Sunday afternoon, was to "promote the exchange of ideas, investigate theories, propagate principles, know the truth, follow an argument wherever it goes and develop ourselves."[15] In addition, although he had not been raised in an especially religious family,[16] Weaver participated enthusiastically in Christian youth activities on campus, serving as an officer (most likely the president) of the Christian Endeavor Society.[17] In 1927, after only three years in residence, he graduated from the Academy as valedictorian of his class.

Weaver's intellectual development continued at the University of Kentucky, where he enrolled as a freshman in the fall of 1927. He first formed a commitment to the cause of world peace as espoused by various Christian youth organizations. In May of 1929 his oration "Our Big Business of War" won top honors in a statewide contest sponsored by the Intercollegiate Peace Association. Seven months later he published his first article, a brief report on the status of the college peace movement in Kentucky for a symposium entitled "A Panorama of Peace" in *The Intercollegian*, a monthly magazine for college students produced by the YMCA and YWCA.[18] From these beginnings, Weaver soon came to embrace the full ideology and agenda of international socialism. One impetus was the campus Liberal Club, which he helped to form in March of 1929 and served thereafter as vice president and president. Although neither large nor particularly active, the club achieved substantial notoriety for its perceived links to the League for Industrial Democracy and its stands on issues such as compulsory military training.[19] In 1932, the year he received his undergraduate degree, Weaver formalized his commitment to socialism by joining the American Socialist Party. Although he later commented that "my disillusionment with the Left began with this first practical step," he served as secretary of the Lexington "local" for about two years and helped to plan an October 1932 campaign appearance in Lexington by Socialist presidential candidate Norman Thomas.[20]

As graduation approached in the spring of 1932, Weaver applied to a number of Southern universities for financial aid to support him in graduate school. He received only one positive response, however, an offer of a small scholarship from the University of Kentucky. Accordingly, in September 1932 he enrolled there as a full-time student in the master's program in English. But the following spring he again applied to other schools for aid, and this time his efforts were rewarded with an offer of a modest scholarship from Vanderbilt. Although it meant repeating most of his graduate course work,[21] Weaver readily accepted the offer and enrolled as a master's student in English at Vanderbilt in the fall of 1933. After completing the master's degree in a single academic year, he enrolled immediately in the doctoral program in English, and by June of 1936 he had completed the course work and all other preliminary requirements for the Ph.D. degree.

The period at Vanderbilt (1933–36) was enormously important in terms of Weaver's intellectual development. As he noted later in his autobiographical essay "Up from Liberalism," he was strongly attracted by the ideals of socialism, but in the course of his work for the Socialist Party he discovered that he did not much care for socialists as persons. In contrast, at Vanderbilt Weaver encountered a number of Southern Agrarians, most notably Robert Penn Warren and John Crowe Ransom (who directed his master's thesis), and found that "although I disagreed with these men on matters of social and political doctrine, I liked them all as persons." As a result, Weaver left Vanderbilt "poised between the two alternatives" of socialism and agrarianism.[22]

It took Weaver four years to fully resolve this dilemma. In the summer of 1936 he left Nashville and began searching for a full-time teaching position to provide financial support while he worked on his dissertation, a study of Milton almost certainly begun under the direction of John Crowe Ransom. But the task of finding a job proved more difficult than anticipated, and by late August Weaver was so desperate that he seriously considered volunteering to fight for the Republican forces in Spain.[23] Finally, at the last possible moment, he was offered a one-year appointment as an instructor in English at the Alabama Polytechnic Institute (now Auburn University) which he accepted with great relief. Despite receiving a renewal of his contract, he began searching again in the spring to find a better job. This eventually produced a very attractive offer of a position as acting assistant professor and director of forensics in the Department of English at Texas A&M University. Clearly delighted, Weaver accepted the appointment and taught there for the next three years (1937–40).

The job at Alabama Polytechnic initiated a period of relative affluence for Weaver which allowed him to indulge his keen interest in travel. In June 1937 he bought his first car, a black, 1934 Ford V-8, which he used to drive between Lexington and College Station, including a memorable 1,500-mile odyssey from Texas to Kentucky via New Orleans, Mobile, Birmingham, Nashville and Louisville at the end of the 1937–38 academic year. Over the Thanksgiving breaks of 1937 and 1938, he drove groups of friends and colleagues to Monterrey, Mexico. In July 1938 he sailed to Europe and spent a month in Paris. And the following year he spent what he described as "the pleasantest summer of my life" studying at Harvard and seeing the sights of New England.[24]

In other respects, however, this was a period of growing discontent for Weaver. Work on the dissertation was not going well, and what little enthusiasm he had for the project dissipated in the summer of 1938 when John Crowe Ransom left Vanderbilt for Kenyon College and was replaced as dissertation director by Claude Finney. It was also at about this time that Weaver finally lost faith in the Left. As he announced in a January 1939 letter to his friend John Randolph: "I am junking Marxism as not founded in experience."[25] That rejection was soon followed by what he later described as "a kind of religious conversion" to the "Church of Agrarianism."[26] Finally, Weaver was becoming increasingly dissatisfied with his job at Texas A&M, in large part because of the attitude of militant scientism and philistinism he encountered there among students and colleagues alike.

These frustrations came to a head in the late summer of 1939. While driving back to Texas after his stay at Harvard, Weaver was transfixed by an epiphanic insight. As he later described the experi-

ence in "Up from Liberalism," "it came to me like a revelation that
I did not *have* to go back to this job, which had become distaste-
ful, and that I did not *have* to go on professing the clichés of liberalism, which were becoming meaningless to me."[27] He therefore
decided to quit his job at the end of the academic year, abandon
the Vanderbilt doctorate and "start my education over."[28] In January 1940 he began the process of applying for admission to the
doctoral program in English at Louisiana State University, where
he hoped to study under Robert Penn Warren, Cleanth Brooks
and others associated with *The Southern Review*. His intentions
were made clear in his application for a graduate fellowship: "My
travels have made me a Southern nationalist rather than an inter-
nationalist, and I now want to do an important piece of research
in the history of my section."[29]

The intellectual origins of *Ideas Have Consequences* can be
traced directly to Weaver's decision to begin his doctoral work
anew at LSU. He enrolled for classes at the Baton Rouge campus
in the fall of 1940, and within six months started writing a new
dissertation under the direction of H. Arlin Turner. The project
was completed in December 1942 under the direction of Cleanth
Brooks, who had assumed that role two months earlier when
Turner was called into military service.

The dissertation is entitled "The Confederate South, 1865–
1910: A Study in the Survival of a Mind and a Culture." It is, by
any measure, a very original and rather peculiar work for a graduate student in English to undertake. As indicated by its subtitle,
it is a study of the mind and culture of the South as articulated
in Southern letters—essays, military memoirs, fiction, diaries and
reminiscences—in the postbellum period. Weaver begins the work
with an analysis of the Southern "heritage," which he reduces to
four principal components.[30] The first is a feudal system of society—derived from Europe but an authentic product of organic
growth—which is, characteristically, stable, agrarian, harmonious
(as opposed to unified) and hierarchical. One consequence of this

organic hierarchy is the existence of a self-conscious aristocratic class. The second component is a code of chivalry, "a romantic idealism closely related to Christianity, which makes honor the guiding principle of conduct," at least among members of the aristocratic class.[31] Third, and closely related to the second, is a system of instruction designed for the education of gentlemen. Intended ultimately to foster the growth of virtue, that education is "moral in the sense that it would give the youth a system of values," and "humanistic" in the sense that it is "so framed as to instill the classic qualities of magnificence, magnanimity, and liberality."[32] Above all, it avoids specialized training, providing instead a "well-rounded regimen" designed to prepare the graduate "to perform all general duties, both public and private, of peace and of war."[33] Last is a distinctive approach to religion, which Weaver calls "the older religiousness," characterized by the simple, unquestioning acceptance of, and willing submission to, a body of religious doctrines. In this view, and in direct contrast to the dominant tradition in New England, religion is less a "reasoned belief" than a "satisfying dogma."[34]

From this heritage have sprung a number of enduring features of the Southern mind and culture. The first is a complex, holistic and nuanced view of reality, marked by a sense of the inscrutable, of the existence of supernatural power, where life is a profound mystery and, because absolutes exist, tragedy is possible. The second is an intellectual posture marked by an appreciation of intuitive, poetic and mythic insight and a corresponding distrust of mere rational intellect and the reductive simplifications of abstract theory and ideology. The third feature is a disdain, even a contempt, for materialism, commercialism and the empty blandishments of an unreflected "progress." Fourth is a natural attitude of piety, which Weaver defines as "the submissiveness of the will, and a general respect for order, natural and institutional."[35] From piety derive such other traits as humility, which involves the recognition and acceptance of proper restraints, and a respect for personality which, almost paradoxically, permits the exaggerated individualism so characteristic of the South.

Although clearly sympathetic to its people and culture, Weaver is no mere apologist for the South. Throughout his analysis he points repeatedly to its faults and excesses, especially a tendency to indulge in an extravagant and sentimental romanticism. And in an "Epilogue" added in 1945 he identifies two "great errors in its struggle against the modern world": a failure to study its position with enough care to discover the philosophical foundation on which its defense could be based, and a progressive loss or "surrender" of initiative.[36] But with all its faults and failures, the South is redeemed by its unique status as *"the last non-materialist civilization in the Western World."*[37] And because of this status, the South can serve a unique and vital function.

> Looking at the whole of the South's promise and achievement, I would be unwilling to say that it offers a foundation, or, because of some accidents of history, even an example. The most that it offers is a challenge. And the challenge is to save the human spirit by re-creating a non-materialist society. Only this can rescue us from a future of nihilism, urged on by the demoniacal force of technology and by our own moral defeatism.[38]

This quotation, like much of the discussion in the "Introduction" and "Epilogue," clearly foreshadows the analysis developed in *Ideas Have Consequences*. But that work was still several years in the future when Weaver graduated from LSU in May of 1943. After a long and frustrating search he eventually secured a position as an instructor in the Army Specialist Training Program at North Carolina State University. But that job lasted only eight months, and by the end of April 1944 he was again looking for work. This time, thanks to the active support of Cleanth Brooks, the outcome was more favorable. On September 6, 1944, Weaver received a telegram from Dean Clarence Faust of the University of Chicago offering a one-year appointment as an English instructor in the undergraduate College. He accepted the offer with evident pleasure and taught at Chicago for the rest of his life.

Despite these distractions, Weaver was able to maintain a substantial program of research and publication in the years immediately following his graduation. Beginning in 1942 while he was still a graduate student at LSU, he submitted for publication a steady stream of essays on Southern subjects derived from his dissertation research, most of them to *The Sewanee Review*. They appeared over the next few years as "The Older Religiousness in the South" (1943), "Albert Taylor Bledsoe" (1944), "The South and the Revolution of Nihilism" (1944) and "Southern Chivalry and Total War" (1945).[39] Weaver also worked steadily at revising his dissertation for publication, especially during his first year at the University of Chicago (1944–45). In July 1945 he took the manuscript to Chapel Hill and spent a week discussing it with the director of the University of North Carolina Press, William Terry Couch, and Couch's assistant, George Scheer. Couch agreed to publish the work if Weaver would add an introduction and epilogue to clarify its focus. That task was completed by the end of the summer.[40]

Although all of Weaver's writings in the period 1941–45 focus on Southern history and culture, it is possible to discern in the later of them—especially the essay "Southern Chivalry and Total War" and the materials added to the dissertation in the summer of 1945—a new and more negative tone. Directed against contemporary American (*i.e.*, Northern) culture, it reflects Weaver's growing revulsion and dismay at American (and Allied) conduct in World War II. This sickened rejection of contemporary culture constitutes the second major strand in Weaver's thinking at the time *Ideas Have Consequences* was written.

The progression of Weaver's views can be seen quite clearly in his comments to his old friends and former Nashville roommates John and Esther Randolph. In January 1942, at the very beginning of hostilities for America, he wrote:

> My outlook for the future is far more pessimistic than yours. I do not want an Axis victory, but I see nothing to hope for through an Allied victory. This idea that peace can be brought about by economic equality is the most fatuous of all delusions. The world is faced with an indefinite period of chaos—years that will be filled with "prison and palace and reverberation" and "torchlight red on sweaty faces." It will not regain order and stability until it returns to the kind of poetic-religious vision of life which dominated the Middle Ages.[41]

At the end of 1942 he declared:

> I am utterly pessimistic about the results of the war. The present ideological alignment is just too phony to last. Here is Churchill, the British imperialist, fighting to free Europe from German national socialism (it is amazing how few people can see that fascism is actually a form of socialism trying, by crude violence, to preserve some of the traditional values). Here we are, serving as "the arsenal of democracy," and pinning our hopes for victory on the fighting power of the most ruthless of all dictatorships, Stalin's Russia. I believe it will appear increasingly that the real war is between Anglo-American rightism and the various forms of European leftism.[42]

Two years later his views had become more thoroughly pessimistic:

> My reaction to the war is even more negative than yours. I have never believed in it, and I believe in it less now than I did in the beginning. This war is not going to improve anything. We are going to get out of it poorer, more disillusioned, more bankrupt in purpose than ever before. . . . The war is like some giant automaton set going by an evil

spirit. Nobody thinks it is creating anything, nobody wants it to go on, but nobody can stop it.[43]

When the war finally did end in August 1945, Weaver's disillusionment was complete:

> Well, the last round of competitive homicide is over, and I have an immense sense of relief. I have really suffered in this war. I have not gone hungry, or gotten cold, or slept without shelter, or felt fright, but I have suffered inwardly. The official lies, the cunningly manipulated hysteria, the repudiation of moral standards by sources we had been taught to respect most—these have been nauseating. . . .
>
> And is anything saved? We cannot be sure. True, there are a few buildings left standing around, but what kind of animal is going to inhabit them? I have become convinced in the past few years that the essence of civilization is ethical (with perhaps some helping out from aesthetics). And never has the power of ethical discrimination been as low as it is today. The atomic bomb was a final blow to the code of humanity. I cannot help thinking that we will suffer retribution for this. For a long time to come I believe my chief interest is going to be the restoration of civilization, of the distinctions that make life intelligible.[44]

In the same letter Weaver proudly announced that it appeared his dissertation would be published by the University of North Carolina Press. But those hopes were soon disappointed. In September 1945 William Terry Couch left North Carolina to become the director of the University of Chicago Press. Although he still felt the dissertation was worthy of publication, Couch informed Weaver that its strong Southern focus precluded him from considering it for the Chicago press.[45] T. J. Wilson, Couch's successor at North Carolina, did ask to review the manuscript and it was sent to him in the spring of 1946. But it was rejected some months later, and Weaver made no further efforts to find a publisher.[46] The reason was that he had begun work on a new manuscript, which eventually appeared as *Ideas Have Consequences*.

It is clear that in the early fall of 1945 Richard Weaver was acutely aware of the contrast between the culture of the South he had described in his dissertation and the culture of contemporary America as revealed especially in the conduct of World War II. It is less evident how that awareness led to the writing of *Ideas Have Consequences*. In "Up from Liberalism" Weaver offers this account of the origins of the book:

> I recall sitting in my office at Ingleside Hall at the University of Chicago one Fall morning in 1945 and wondering whether it would not be possible to deduce, from fundamental causes, the fallacies of modern life and thinking that had produced this holocaust and would insure others. In about twenty minutes I jotted down a series of chapter headings, and this was the inception of a book entitled *Ideas Have Consequences*.[47]

While this may very well provide an accurate account of how the structure of the book was determined, there is strong evidence that the idea for such a work was first suggested in a meeting in Couch's Chicago apartment attended by Weaver, Couch and Cleanth Brooks, who was a visiting professor at the University of Chicago during the Autumn and Winter quarters of the 1945–46 academic year. For example, in a May 1948 letter to Brooks about the reception accorded to *Ideas Have Consequences*, Weaver begins:

> I don't want to burden you with more correspondence, but since the idea we concocted at Couch's three years ago has created a mighty splash, you will probably be interested in hearing some details from this end.[48]

The content of that discussion is suggested by Weaver's comment in a July 1946 letter to Arlin Turner:

> I have seen a good bit of Couch at Chicago, and he has suggested that if I will take the conclusions of the dissertation and apply them in a general way to the modern world, I might produce a work in which the Chicago Press is interested.[49]

Regardless of the details of its inception, it is clear that Weaver began work on the new book in October or November of 1945 and produced a volume very much in line with Couch's suggestion. The finished work shows an obvious affinity with many of the main ideas of Weaver's dissertation and clear indications of the revulsion he felt toward the modern world in the aftermath of the Second World War. But the arguments in *Ideas Have Consequences* go substantially beyond his views in 1945 and show the mark of other influences as well.

The first of these is Weaver's reaction against what he called the posture of "systemic relativism" that permeated the undergraduate liberal arts curriculum at Chicago, especially as expounded by Richard McKeon in the capstone Observation, Interpretation and Integration (OII) course.[50] In this view, the pursuit of truth is limited to arraying different viewpoints nonreductively, systematizing their assumptions and methods, and proceeding within their confines. The problem with this approach is that it tends to foster a kind of brilliant but empty dialectical virtuosity. Nevertheless, Weaver did profit from his exposure to the position and its proponents, as indicated by a comment in a July 1946 letter to Arlin Turner. Regarding an early draft of the book he wrote:

> Some of the first chapters deal with metaphysics, for experience with these gifted Chicago dialecticians has taught me that there is no sense in going ahead until you have clarified your philosophical foundations.[51]

A second influence was his work in the English 3 course, which he taught for the first time in the 1945–46 academic year. In the spring of 1946 Weaver and several other young instructors argued successfully for a major revision of the course, to include, among other changes, a greater emphasis on logic and the informal fallacies.[52] His work in these areas led him to consider for the first time the implications of Occam's Razor and the nature and limits of pure dialectic.

Other influences can be traced to specific individuals, of whom three are most important. The first of these is Pierre Albert Duhamel.[53] Duhamel arrived at Chicago in the fall of 1945 after completing his doctorate at the University of Wisconsin and was assigned to share an office with Weaver. Although Duhamel was married, his wife soon contracted pneumonia and returned to Wisconsin to recuperate with her family. Thus thrown together, Duhamel and Weaver became very close friends.

It was Weaver's habit to return home after lunch each day to write a page or two. He would then discuss his progress with Duhamel in their office that afternoon. The two also met frequently at Duhamel's home on Saturday nights to discuss great ideas over a gallon of Lowenbrau beer (an endeavor in which they were sometimes joined by Cleanth Brooks and Marshall McLuhan). So close was their friendship that when Duhamel returned to Wisconsin to visit his wife's family over spring break of 1946, he invited Weaver to come along. They stayed together at the University Club and spent their evenings drinking beer in Duhamel's old haunts on State Street in Madison.

The key factor in their intellectual relationship was that Duhamel, who received his undergraduate degree from Holy Cross, brought Weaver into contact with a Roman Catholic intellectual tradition that was largely new to him. As a result, their conversations often focused on Medieval Catholic philosophers such as Occam, but also such figures as Duns Scotus and Bonaventura (although seldom Aquinas, for whom Weaver apparently felt an aversion). Duhamel also introduced Weaver to the works of modern Catholic writers such as Eric Gill and Gerard Manley Hopkins. These contacts with Duhamel are almost certainly the source of the undertone of Roman Catholicism that many readers have noted in *Ideas Have Consequences*.

Thanks partly to Duhamel's tutelage, Weaver made steady progress on the manuscript over the course of the 1945–46 academic year. However, the bulk of the first draft was written during the summer of 1946. Weaver spent that period in residence at the University of Wisconsin, where, at Duhamel's suggestion, he enrolled in a single course in Greek to facilitate his understanding of the works of the early Greek rhetorical theorists. But most of his time was devoted to writing. By July he had completed a chapter outline that lists most of the arguments included in the finished work but lacks the discussion of Occam and nominalism now found in the "Introduction."[54] On October 26, he sent a completed first draft to Couch with a plea for criticism. The manuscript was entitled "Steps Toward a Restoration of Our World."[55]

The initial response to the manuscript was highly enthusiastic, as Weaver related in a January 1947 letter to Cleanth Brooks:

> The first reaction from this quarter astonished me completely. Couch invited me to Thanksgiving dinner, talked about little else, declared that this was "the finest piece of writing that I have received since I took over the Press here." That nearly bowled me over, but it is exactly what he said. His chief editor, Frederick Wieck, talked in similar vein, and described one of the chapters as "wonderful." Can you blame anyone for assuming, as I did then, that not much stood in the way of publication?[56]

However, as Weaver's plaintive question suggests, the book soon encountered what he described as "reader trouble." Although reviews by Cleanth Brooks and Otto von Simson recommended publication, those by E. K. Brown and Marjorie Greve were highly negative. As Weaver noted: "There are in the work certain phrases, perhaps ideas, which cause readers simply to explode."[57] But even the positive reviews pointed out many deficiencies, and in January 1947 Weaver was asked to revise the work.

A key figure in this process was Cleanth Brooks. It is ironic that Brooks is generally given credit for shaping Weaver's dissertation (published posthumously as *The Southern Tradition at Bay*). In fact, Brooks had little influence on that work, which was almost finished when he took over as dissertation director. But he did play a major role in shaping and refining *Ideas Have Consequences*. He was present at the meeting with Weaver and Couch where the idea for the book was first discussed, and he worked informally with Weaver in the earliest stages of the project to help formulate his major arguments. In the spring of 1947 he provided a set of detailed suggestions which Weaver gratefully incorporated into the text. Weaver acknowledged his influence in a letter dated May 1, 1947:

> With reference to the points of criticism, I may say that I agree with every one of them. I realized that I was on shakiest ground in my discussion of the arts, though I did do a fair amount of patient research up in Madison last summer.[58]

Three weeks later Weaver wrote:

> How *Ideas Have Consequences* Came to Be Written
> In re the manuscript: I have decided to overhaul completely the chapters on the arts and on language. And since my vein is flowing rather happily at the moment, I think I am effecting some solid improvements. I was appalled when after an interval of two months I looked again at the part on literature and language and saw how skimpy I had left it. Certainly the mood of creation is not the mood of criticism.[59]

Weaver completed the revisions in June of 1947. Armed with additional favorable reviews from Joseph Rotskoff and Alburey Castell, Couch submitted it to the press committee the following month. On July 11, the manuscript was formally accepted, and a week later Weaver was issued a contract for publication of the work, now entitled "The Adverse Descent."[60]

Once the contract was signed, the fate of the book was passed to the capable hands of William Terry Couch. It would be difficult to overestimate the significance of Couch's role in this endeavor. He may well have made the initial suggestion for the work, and he guided the manuscript through the long process of writing, review, and revision. Now he would add his stamp in at least three other ways.

The first was his decision to throw the full weight of the University of Chicago Press behind the book.[61] The initial press run was set in August at 3,500 copies. But as the reader reports and endorsements accumulated, Couch was impressed by the extremely intense responses—both positive and negative—the book tended to generate. This suggested that it could well be as controversial, and as profitable, as Hayek's *Road to Serfdom*. He therefore increased the initial printing to 4,000 copies in September and to 7,500 copies in December, with provisions for a second printing of equal size. He also authorized an advertising budget of $7,500, an extraordinary amount for a book with a retail price of $2.75.

Couch's second major contribution was to work tirelessly to secure prominent endorsements for the book. Some individuals, such as C. S. Lewis, declined to comment, citing the pressure of other obligations. Others responded with harsh criticism. For example, Philip Wylie commented:

> I have now read *Ideas Have Consequences* and I am passionately unimpressed by the book; while I still believe in the title, I think that for any valid consequences, real ideas are necessary, and I find in this

volume an almost total absence of any ideas save a few odds and ends
the author has borrowed and then misunderstood. I have assigned this
dreary little volume a place in my bookcase behind the other books so
that it will by no chance have the consequence of boring or confusing
any of my guests or friends.[62]

But in the end Couch was able to assemble an impressive array
of endorsements from such notable figures as Cleanth Brooks,
John Abbot Clark, Donald Davidson, Norman Foerster, Charles
Clayton Morrison, Reinhold Niebuhr, Melvin Rader, John Crowe
Ransom, Allen Tate, and Paul Tillich. These were duly featured on
the dust jackets and in the advertising campaign.

But perhaps Couch's greatest contribution was the title of the
book. He first suggested *Ideas Have Consequences* in a memorandum dated October 4, 1947. Six days later Fred Wieck reported
that Weaver "had come around to the view that this title was very
strong," and stressed that "I did not have to force the title down
his throat, nor did I have to bludgeon him into swallowing it. His
statement expresses his sincere conviction."[63] Despite these claims,
it is clear that Weaver deeply disliked the title, and his resentment
erupted in an angry public exchange with Couch at a party on
October 25. In the heat of the moment Weaver apparently went
so far as to suggest he might withdraw the book from the Press,
and Couch responded with a formal offer to release him from his
contract. Fortunately for all concerned, Weaver reconsidered his
position, and the next day sent Couch a written apology for "my
rudeness at the party." He explained:

> For some time I have been conscious of violating my own prescript—
> that is to say, I have been conscious of becoming egotistic about the
> book in question, of attaching to it an importance which it does not
> have. That may account for an exaggerated sensitivity about titles and
> other things. I ought to take more of my own advice and get a perspec-
> tive on things.[64]

That matter settled, the book went smoothly into press. But the result was that a phrase that Weaver later described as "hopelessly banal"[65] has now become indissolubly linked with his name.

———

The fate of the book and its author were left hanging in the balance some pages ago, and it remains to discuss how they fared. In the end, *Ideas Have Consequences* met neither the fondest expectations nor the darkest fears of those who brought it into being. Most likely as a result of both the less than inspired advertising campaign and a number of prominent negative reviews such as those by Jones and Wecter, it generated only relatively modest sales. Couch had hoped that as many as 30,000 copies would be bought. But by mid-1948 the total stood at less than 8,000,[66] and in the following year returns outnumbered sales by a ratio of almost two to one.[67] As Couch noted in a letter in July 1948:

> *Ideas Have Consequences* has had at least one serious consequence for me. It has lost us a fair sized chunk of money, and I am now discovering that dollars make a lot of difference to this place. Unless I am able to get rid of some of the sacred cows around here it will be a long time before I will be able to take any long chances like this again.[68]

As far as Richard Weaver is concerned, the fears for his job proved groundless. In fact, just three months after the book was published he was promoted from instructor to assistant professor and issued a three-year contract, the first multi-year contract he had received in 12 years of teaching. And despite some incidents of petty harassment and the evident disdain of certain colleagues, he went on to enjoy a conventionally successful academic career at Chicago. More important, *Ideas Have Consequences* established Weaver as a leader in the fledgling conservative movement, a status he held until his death in 1963.

Finally, it must be noted that Couch's pessimistic conclusion was perhaps a bit premature. Although not an immediate bestseller, orders for copies of the second printing continued at a respectable rate through the end of 1958, when stocks were at last exhausted and the book was declared out of print.[69] But demand for the book continued, and within a matter of months the Press decided to reissue it in paperback under its Phoenix imprint. The new edition was duly published in late 1959 or early 1960,[70] and by August 1960 more than 3,000 copies had been sold.[71] And *Ideas Have Consequences* has remained in print continuously ever since.

ACKNOWLEDGMENTS

The author expresses thanks to the following publishers and authors for permission to make use of material from their publications:

The Cambridge University Press (quotation by permission of the Macmillan Company, publishers, New York) for the quotation from *The Future in Education*, by Sir Richard Livingstone; Dodd, Mead and Company for the quotation from *Modern Painting*, by Willard Huntington Wright; Doubleday and Company, Inc., for the quotations from *Jazz*, by Robert Goffin; Faber and Faber, Ltd., for the quotation from *Music Ho!*, by Constant Lambert; Harcourt, Brace and Company for the quotations from *Language in Action*, by S. I. Hayakawa; Mr. Norman H. Hinton for the quotation from *Political Semantics*; Kegan Paul, Trench, Trubner and Company, Ltd., for the quotation from *The Spirit of Language in Civilization*, by Karl Vossler; Alfred A. Knopf, Inc., for the quotation from *The American Democrat*, by James Fenimore Cooper; Mr. Alfred Korzybski for the quotation from *Science and Sanity*; the Macmillan Company for the quotation from *Language and Reality*, by W. M. Urban, and for the quotations from *The Collected Poems of William Butler Yeats*; Pantheon Books, Inc., for the quotation from *Force and Freedom*, by Jacob Burckhardt; G. P. Putnam's Sons and Eyre and Spottiswoode, Ltd., for the quotation from *Men of Chaos* (published in Great Britain as *Makers of Destruction*), by Hermann Rauschning; the Yale University Press for the quotations from *The Folklore of Capitalism*, by Thurman Arnold; and the Ziff-Davis Publishing Company for the quotation from *The Redemption of Democracy*, by Hermann Rauschning.

Richard M. Weaver
The University of Chicago

NOTES

FOREWORD TO THE EXPANDED EDITION

1. Readers of Allan Bloom's *The Closing of the American Mind* will recall Bloom's equally vigorous assault on rock music as a purveyor of "premature ecstasy" that "artificially produces the exaltation naturally attached to the completion of the greatest endeavors—victory in a just war, consummated love, artistic creation, religious devotion and discovery of the truth."

CHAPTER 1

1. From *The Collected Poems of W. B. Yeats*. By permission of the Macmillan Company, publishers.

CHAPTER 2

1. I have here characterized the materialism underlying the main stream of socialist thinking, but it is only fair to add that there are differing conceptions. There is, for example, the "socialist poverty" of the French poet, Charles Péguy; and the German General von Blomberg in a conversation with Hermann Rauschning could identify socialism with Prussian discipline. "Prussianism was always Socialism," he said, "because Prussianism means poverty and discipline. Prussianism means being hard to oneself and to others, but chiefly to oneself. Prussianism means happiness in work and satisfaction in service. Prussianism means living and dying in harness" (from *Men of Chaos*, copyright, 1942, by Hermann Rauschning. Courtesy of G. P. Putnam's Sons).

2. Norman Thomas has put this in the form of a dilemma by asking whether Roosevelt was justified in taking the American people into the second World War against their will and knowledge. If he was, then the leader is something apart

from the masses, not merely the executor of their wishes, and thus we have again the ancient dichotomy of ruler and ruled.

CHAPTER 3

1. George Santayana, interviewed in Rome after its capture by American troops, declared that Mussolini had done as much for the city as the two Napoleons had done for Paris but that "definitely he was not a gentleman."

CHAPTER 4

1. Constant Lambert, *Music Ho!* p. 179.

2. In Ravel, music offers a parallel to Cézanne, whom I shall discuss at the end of the chapter; for Ravel, after a period of absorption, so to speak, in subject matter, turned back toward "clarity of thought and sobriety of form."

3. Robert Goffin, *Jazz*, p. 42.

4. *Ibid.*, p. 5.

5. Willard Huntington Wright, *Modern Painting*, p. 84.

CHAPTER 5

1. A different but more serious question is what percentage of genuine tragedies could be identified as tragedies by a modern audience? For the inability of the contemporary mind to recognize tragedy when it is presented, see Robert B. Heilman's "Melpomene as Wallflower," *Sewanee Review*, winter, 1947.

2. It is a fact in keeping with others which we have cited that rural and urban tastes in radio differ. An official survey made by the Bureau of Agricultural Economics found that whereas with city people "comedy-variety shows are the overwhelming favorites, rural people generally seemed to prefer the more serious type of programs, such as news and market reports, religious music and sermons."

3. In his novel *The Bostonians*, which deserves to be better known, Henry James sends the "southern" type of mind into a northern environment, with consequences that corroborate Page's thesis.

4. An anthropologist related to me that certain Negro tribes of West Africa have a symbol for the white man consisting of a figure seated on the deck of a steamer in a position of stiffest rigidity. The straight, uncompromising lines are the betrayal; the primitive artist has caught the white man's unnatural rigor, which contrasts, ominously for him, with the native's sinuous adaptation.

A mind nurtured on press, motion picture, and radio cannot be otherwise in relation to the complexity of the world. Its instructors do not teach it to use the "proper reticences and proprieties" toward different things, and so its ideas may be comical simplifications.

CHAPTER 7

1. It seems an inescapable conclusion that the New Deal's practice of making special investigations of the income-tax payments of individuals and groups which opposed it is an instance of trend toward economic excommunication.

2. Andrew D. White, *Fiat Money in France* (1896), p. 79.

3. The most striking illustration is the Spanish phrase for corporation, *sociedad anénima*.

CHAPTER 8

1. *Language in Action*, p. 121.

2. *Ibid.*, p. 63.

3. Norman H. Hinton, *Political Semantics*, p. 68.

4. It may be objected at this point that I have chosen to deal only with the popularizers of semantics, with men who have cheapened or distorted the science. Because this work is a study in social consequences, it is necessary to look at the form in which these doctrines reach the public. There is, of course, a group of serious philosophers who are working at language with caution and a sense of responsibility and who believe that they are erecting for us important safeguards against error. But, when I look into the writings of these men, I find, alas, that their conclusions march in the same direction as those of the popularizers. The Darwinian link is acknowledged, and semantics resembles, as much as before, behaviorism imported into language. Thus Charles W. Morris in *Foundations of the Theory of Signs* stresses the importance of semantics because "it has directed attention more closely to the relation of signs to their users than had previously been done and has assessed more profoundly than ever before the relevance of this relation in understanding intellectual activities." Language is spoken of as if it were some curious development of sense which enables an organism to take into account objects not perceptually present. The determination of the scientist to see all reality as process appears later in the same work when Morris collapses the notion of "meaning" by making it purely a function of relationships. That is to say, nothing is, intrinsically, but each thing is, in terms of the process as a whole. The significant implication follows that concepts are not entities but are, rather, highly selective processes "in which the organism gets indications as to how to act with reference to the world in order to satisfy its needs or interests."

5. *Language and Reality*, p. 241. By permission of the Macmillan Company, publishers.

6. I feel certain that the Reverend John Robinson had a similar thought in

mind when he enjoined the Plymouth Pilgrims to look upon their civil leaders "not beholding in them the ordinarinesse of their persons, but God's ordinance for your own good."

7. *The Future in Education* (Cambridge University Press, England), pp. 109–10. By permission of the Macmillan Company, publishers.

CHAPTER 9

1. From *The Collected Poems of W. B. Yeats*. By permission of the Macmillan Company, publishers.

AFTERWORD

1. Undated and unsigned typescript sheet headed "Richard M. Weaver IDEAS HAVE CONSEQUENCES." Located in Box 483, File 6, of the University of Chicago Press Records in the Special Collections of the Regenstein Library at the University of Chicago and quoted by permission.

2. University of Chicago Press advertisement, *Publishers' Weekly* (January 17, 1948), 206–07.

3. Form letter from W. T. Couch dated January 22, 1948. Located in Box 483, File 5, of the University of Chicago Press Records and quoted by permission.

4. University of Chicago Press advertisement, *Publishers' Weekly* (February 21, 1948), 1036.

5. Letter from Donald B. Barnes to Jocelyn Kahn dated March 19, 1948. Located in Box 483, File 5, of the University of Chicago Press Records and quoted by permission.

6. See, *e.g., The Saturday Review of Literature* (March 6, 1948), 7, and (March 20, 1948), 3.

7. Letter from Richard Weaver to Robert Heilman dated July 2, 1948. Located in the Robert Heilman Papers in the Manuscripts and University Archives Division of the University of Washington Libraries and quoted by permission.

8. Letter from Richard Weaver to Cleanth Brooks dated January 28, 1948. Located in Box 15, Folder 320, of the Cleanth Brooks Papers in the Beinecke Rare Book and Manuscript Library at Yale University.

9. Letter from Richard Weaver to Cleanth Brooks dated May 31, 1948. Located in Box 15, Folder 320, of the Cleanth Brooks Papers.

10. The details of Dick and Carrye's relationship are confirmed by correspondence and other documents acquired from Weaver's sister, Polly Weaver Beaton, and now in the author's possession. See also the entry on them in Pearl M. Weaver, *The Tribe of Jacob* (Asheville: Miller Printing, 1962), 112. Additional

confirmation was provided by William Embry, Jr., in a telephone interview conducted by the author on January 4, 1996.

11. From a local newspaper obituary dated December 17, 1915, acquired from Mrs. Polly Weaver Beaton and now in the author's possession.

12. Telephone interview with William Embry, Jr., January 4, 1996.

13. For a brief description of his earliest educational experiences, see Richard M. Weaver, *The Role of Education in Shaping Our Society* (Bryn Mawr: Intercollegiate Studies Institute, undated pamphlet), 10.

14. Interview with Mrs. Dee Amyx conducted in Lexington, Kentucky, on January 23, 1997.

15. From the handwritten "Charter" of the society acquired from Mrs. Polly Weaver Beaton and now in the author's possession. The fullest account of Weaver's activities at the Academy is found in his unpublished 1958 eulogy "William Maury Mitchell," which is included in a comprehensive collection of Weaver's shorter writings forthcoming from Liberty Press in 1999.

16. Interviews with Embry Lee Weaver and Polly Weaver Beaton conducted in Weaverville, North Carolina, on August 11, 1995.

17. The nature and extent of Weaver's participation in the Christian Endeavor Society are indicated by a number of entries (including two speeches and four prayers prepared for oral presentation at meetings) in a notebook of his from that period acquired from Mrs. Polly Weaver Beaton and now in the author's possession. For extensive excerpts from that notebook, see Fred Douglas Young, *Richard M. Weaver 1910–1963: A Life of the Mind* (Columbia: University of Missouri Press, 1995), 18–20.

18. See "Richard Weaver Is Winner in Contest," *Kentucky Kernel* (May 24, 1929), 8; "Richard Weaver Wins Peace Prize," *Lexington Leader* (May 24, 1929); and Richard M. Weaver, "Kentucky," in "A Panorama of Peace: A Symposium," *The Intercollegian* 47 (December 1929), 72.

19. For a detailed discussion of the Liberal Club and Weaver's early political views, see Clifford Amyx, "Weaver the Liberal," *Modern Age* 31 (Spring 1987), 101–06. See also the file of newspaper clippings on the Liberal Club in the Archives of the University of Kentucky.

20. Richard M. Weaver, "Up from Liberalism," *Modern Age* 3 (Winter 1958–59), 22.

21. An examination of Weaver's transcripts from Kentucky and Vanderbilt shows that only one course from his year of work at Kentucky was accepted as transfer credit for his master's degree at Vanderbilt.

22. Weaver, "Up from Liberalism," 23.

23. Letter from Richard Weaver to John Randolph dated August 23, 1936, from a copy in the author's possession. The discussion of Weaver's activities in the period 1936–40 is based primarily on his correspondence with his close friends John and Esther Randolph, with whom he shared an apartment during his last year at Vanderbilt.

24. Letter from Richard Weaver to John Randolph dated August 12, 1939. Quoted by permission of Mrs. Esther Randolph.

25. Letter from Richard Weaver to John Randolph dated January 26, 1939. Quoted by permission of Mrs. Esther Randolph.

26. Letter from Richard Weaver to John Randolph dated January 20, 1942. Quoted by permission of Mrs. Esther Randolph.

27. Weaver, "Up from Liberalism," 24.

28. *Ibid.*

29. Richard M. Weaver, Application for Fellowship to the Graduate School of The Louisiana State University, undated, p. 3. Located in the Richard M. Weaver file in the Department of English Records, RG# A0607, Louisiana State University Archives, LSU Libraries, Baton Rouge, Louisiana, and quoted by permission.

30. Richard M. Weaver, *The Southern Tradition at Bay*, ed. George Core and M.E. Bradford (Washington: Regnery Gateway, 1989 [1968]), 31–95.

31. *Ibid.*, 31.

32. *Ibid.*, 61–62.

33. *Ibid.*, 63.

34. *Ibid.*, 82–83.

35. *Ibid.*, 82.

36. *Ibid.*, 373–74.

37. *Ibid.*, 375, emphasis in original.

38. *Ibid.*

39. Richard M. Weaver, "The Older Religiousness in the South," *The Sewanee Review* 51 (April 1943), 237–49; "Albert Taylor Bledsoe," *The Sewanee Review* 52 (Winter 1944), 34–45; "The South and the Revolution of Nihilism," *The South Atlantic Quarterly* 43 (April 1944), 194–98; and "Southern Chivalry and Total War," *The Sewanee Review* 53 (Spring 1945), 159–70. All of these have been reprinted in *The Southern Essays of Richard M. Weaver*, ed. George M. Curtis III and James J. Thompson, Jr. (Indianapolis: Liberty Press, 1987). At least one essay, "The Anatomy of Southern Failure," was submitted to *The Sewanee Review* in 1944 but rejected. An edited version of this essay will appear in the comprehensive collection of Weaver's shorter writings forthcoming from Liberty Press in 1999.

40. For a description of Weaver's meeting with Couch, see his letter to Cleanth Brooks dated July 9, 1945, in Box 15, Folder 320, of the Cleanth Brooks Papers.

41. Weaver to Randolph, January 20, 1942, quoted by permission.

42. Letter from Richard Weaver to John Randolph dated December 27, 1942. Quoted by permission of Mrs. Esther Randolph.

43. Letter from Richard Weaver to John Randolph dated January 16, 1945. Quoted by permission of Mrs. Esther Randolph.

44. Letter from Richard Weaver to John Randolph dated August 24, 1945. Quoted by permission of Mrs. Esther Randolph.

45. See the letter from Richard Weaver to Arlin Turner dated July 3, 1946, located in the Richard Weaver file in the Arlin Turner Papers (2nd 84:A) in the Special Collections Library at Duke University.

46. According to Louis H. T. Dehmlow in an interview with the author conducted in Wilmette, Illinois, on November 1, 1992, the envelope containing the returned manuscript lay unopened in a corner of Weaver's office until after his death, when it was discovered by Dehmlow. It was eventually published in 1968 as *The Southern Tradition at Bay*.

47. Weaver, "Up from Liberalism," 30.

48. Weaver to Brooks, May 31, 1948.

49. Weaver to Turner, July 3, 1946, quoted by permission.

50. It would be more accurate (and charitable) to label McKeon's perspective "skeptical pluralism." For a detailed explication and application of this approach, see Ted J. Smith III, "Diversity and Order in Communication Theory: The Uses of Philosophical Analysis," *Communication Quarterly* 36 (1988), 28–40.

51. Weaver to Turner, July 3, 1946, quoted by permission.

52. See, *e.g.*, Weaver's letter to Cleanth Brooks dated April 25, 1946. Located in Box 15, Folder 320, of the Cleanth Brooks Papers.

53. The account that follows is based on interviews with Duhamel conducted in Boston, Massachusetts, on May 17 and November 11, 1994.

54. See the eight-page typescript headed "Weaver, Richard M." and date-stamped July 31, 1946, located in Box 483, Folder 5, of the University of Chicago Press Records.

55. See the Letter from Richard Weaver to William Couch dated October 26, 1946. Located in Box 483, Folder 5, of the University of Chicago Press Records.

56. Letter from Richard Weaver to Cleanth Brooks dated January 13, 1947. Located in Box 15, Folder 320, of the Cleanth Brooks Papers.

57. *Ibid.*

58. Letter from Richard Weaver to Cleanth Brooks dated May 1, 1947. Located in Box 15, Folder 320, of the Cleanth Brooks Papers.

59. Letter from Richard Weaver to Cleanth Brooks dated May 24, 1947. Located in Box 15, Folder 320, of the Cleanth Brooks Papers.

60. As noted by Joseph Scotchie, *Barbarians in the Saddle* (New Brunswick: Transaction, 1997), 58, the exact wording of this title has been the subject of some controversy. The wording used here is confirmed by a signed copy of the original contract acquired from Mrs. Polly Weaver Beaton and now in the author's possession. An unsigned copy of the contract can be found in Box 483, Folder 5, of the University of Chicago Press Records.

61. The discussion that follows is based on various documents located in Box 483, Folders 5 and 6, of the University of Chicago Press Records.

62. Letter from Philip Wylie to Elizabeth L. Titus dated April 16, 1948. Located in Box 483, Folder 5, of the University of Chicago Press Records and quoted by permission.

63. Memorandum from FW (Fred Wieck) to DB and EW dated October 10, 1947. Located in Box 483, Folder 6, of the University of Chicago Press Records and quoted by permission.

64. Letter from Richard Weaver to William Couch dated October 26, 1947. Located in Folder 27 of the William T. Couch Papers in the Southern Historical Collection of the Library of the University of North Carolina at Chapel Hill and quoted by permission.

65. Weaver to Heilman, July 2, 1948, quoted by permission.

66. *Ibid.*

67. Letter from Ethel Kellstrom to Richard Weaver dated August 26, 1949. Located in Box 483, Folder 5, of the University of Chicago Press Records.

68. Letter from William Couch to Selma Fuller dated July 13, 1948. Located in Folder 29 of the William T. Couch Papers and quoted by permission.

69. Although the book was technically out of print, as late as June 1959 the Press still had a number of slightly damaged copies which it was selling at a discount of 40%. See, *e.g.*, the letter from Jo Anne Schlag to Stephen Miles dated June 10, 1959, and located in Box 483, Folder 9, of the University of Chicago Press Records.

70. The uncertainty about the publication date stems from the fact that the Phoenix reprint carries no unambiguous year of publication. Weaver's "Foreword" is marked "September 1959," and that is the date which appears in standard catalogue entries, including the Library of Congress. However, a number of items of Weaver's correspondence strongly suggest that the book was not issued

until February or March of 1960. See, *e.g.*, the memorandum from William Wood to Richard Weaver dated March 16, 1960, located in Box 483, Folder 9, of the University of Chicago Press Records.

71. See the letter from William Wood to Richard Weaver dated August 22, 1960, located in Box 483, Folder 9, of the University of Chicago Press Records.